THE
K I D'S

GUIDE TO
DENVER, BOULDER &
COLORADO'S SKI COUNTRY

D1503594

Eileen Ogintz

gpp®

Guilford, Connecticut
Helena, Montana
An imprint of Rowman & Littlefield

Thank you to Melanie Yemma for her insights and fact-checking; to Meghan McCloskey, Jonathan Boydston, Colorado Kids reporters, and Nick Hanle for their reporting; and to Colorado teachers Jackie Burt, Mariell Dick-Valdez, Hallie Harrison, and Tiffni Rule and the students at Orsh School in Gunnison, CO, Aspen Middle School in Aspen, CO, Taylor Elementary School in Colorado Springs, CO, and Stober North Elementary School in Golden, CO. Thank you also to the museum staffs at the Denver Art Museum and Denver Museum of Nature & Science who also helped me gain insights from kids about their institutions.

Globe Pequot is an imprint of Rowman & Littlefield

Distributed by NATIONAL BOOK NETWORK

Copyright © 2015 Eileen Ogintz
Illustrations licensed by Shutterstock.com

British Library Cataloguing in Publication Information available

Library of Congress Cataloging-in-Publication Data available

ISBN 978-1-4930-0643-4 (paperback)

∞™ The paper used in this publication meets the minimum requirements of American National Standard for Information Sciences—Permanence of Paper for Printed Library Materials, ANSI/NISO Z39.48-1992.

All the information in this guidebook is subject to change. We recommend that you call ahead to obtain current information before traveling.

Contents

1

Welcome to Denver

WATCH YOUR STEP!

You don't want to miss being exactly a mile high.

You will be in downtown Denver—if you stop on the 13th step of the west side of the State Capitol Building downtown. There's a brass marker there, telling you that you are exactly 5,280 feet above sea level.

That's why Denver is called the Mile-High City. But even experts make mistakes—and need kids to set them straight. At first, they thought the 15th step marked 1 mile. You can see the step carved with "One Mile High." But then some college kids, using GPS equipment, figured out the correct mile-high elevation was at the 13th step.

DID YOU KNOW?

The Native Americans warned early settlers not to build where Denver is now. But no one listened and in its first few years, Denver was destroyed twice by fire and flood.

In Denver you'll find great kid-friendly museums, fun restaurants, and lots of shopping. But you'll want to spend much of your time outdoors like local kids and their parents do—hiking, biking, tubing in summer, and skiing and snowboarding in the mountains nearby in the winter. Did you know Denver has one of the biggest skate parks in the country?

This city has come a long way from the mining camp established during the "Pikes Peak or Bust" Gold Rush in 1858. In those first years, Denver survived a flood, two big fires, Native American attacks, and even an invading Confederate force of soldiers during the Civil War. But

A COLORADO KID SAYS:
"If you're visiting Colorado for the first time, be ready for a great time full of fun and adventure!"
—Mark, 11, Denver

within 50 years, Denver had become the "Queen City of the Plains," the fanciest city within a thousand miles complete with big mansions and tree-lined avenues. Think about that transformation as you look around the big, modern city Denver is today.

There are fun neighborhoods to explore. Make sure you get the names right:

- The Golden Triangle Museum District includes the super-kid-friendly Denver Art Museum (100 W. 14th Ave. Pkwy., Denver, CO; 720-865-5000; denverart museum.org), the US Mint (320 W. Colfax Ave., Denver, CO; 303-405-4761; usmint.gov), and the interactive History Colorado Center (1200 Broadway, Denver, CO; 303-447-8679; historycolorado.org), among others.

DID YOU KNOW?

Denver has the largest city park system in the country—205 parks and 20,000 more acres of parklands in the mountains where you can play, bike, hike, and more!

- Uptown just east of downtown and including 17th Street is known for its restaurants.

- The Art District on Santa Fe (between 5th Avenue and 10th Avenue) is where you can peek into art galleries— especially on the First Friday night of the month when they're all open. You'll find some of the city's best Mexican restaurants and the Museo de las Americas, which showcases art from South and Central America. Come at the holidays to see all the decorations!

A VISITING KID SAYS:
"You can get cool postcards of pictures from all around the city."
—Marcus, 11, Los Angeles, CA

- The Riverfront/Platte River Valley is where you'll find Elitch Gardens Theme and Water Park (2000 Elitch Circle, Denver, CO; 303-595-4386; elitchgardens.com), the Children's Museum of Denver (2121 Children's Museum Dr., Denver, CO; 303-433-7444; mychilds museum.org), and the Downtown Aquarium (700 Water St., Denver, CO; 303-561-4450; aquarium restaurants.com).

- LoDo stands for Lower Downtown—the 25 blocks north of Larimer Street. You'll come here to go to Coors Field to see the Colorado Rockies play, but while you're in the neighborhood, check out all the interesting old buildings—the biggest concentration of turn-of-the-20th-century architecture anywhere in the country.

Got the lingo? Now you just have to decide where to go first!

DID YOU KNOW?

More than a million people have moved to Colorado in the last decade. Now more people live in Denver than in the entire state of Wyoming.

Staying Safe on Vacation

Write down the name and phone number of the hotel where you are staying. Also write down your parents' phone numbers—or make sure they are in your phone. Carry these numbers with you wherever you go.

Practice "what if" situations with your parents. What should you do if you get lost in a museum? A theme park? On a city street?

Only ask uniformed people for help if you get lost—police officers, firefighters, store security guards, or museum officials wearing official badges.

Wherever you go, decide on a central and easy-to-locate spot to meet in case you get separated.

A VISITING KID SAYS:
"Whenever I'm sightseeing I always have my phone with me so I can take cool pictures and find my friends or parents if we get separated."
—Savannah, 8, Tiffin, OH

High Altitude Smarts

In Denver you're a mile above sea level and when you get to the mountains, you're a lot higher. That means the air is thinner. Here's how kids and their parents in Denver and around Colorado compensate:

- Drink twice as much water as you do at home. That helps your body adjust, especially because the air is drier here.

- Eat foods high in potassium like bananas, avocado, broccoli, granola, dried fruit, and tomatoes.

- Don't play as hard! The effects of exercise are a lot more intense here.

- Wear sunscreen, sunglasses, and lip balm. There's 25 percent less protection from the sun so you'll really need them!

- Dress in layers. Because you're closer to the sun, you may feel warmer than the temperature suggests you should during the day, but you'll get cold at night.

What People Get Wrong About Denver

- Denver isn't in the West, though a lot of people dress like cowboys. It's smack in the middle of the country, closest to the exact center of the nation than any other major metropolitan area except for Kansas City.

- Denver isn't in the mountains; it's near them, at the foot of the Rockies on the high plains. The foothills don't start to rise until 15 miles west of the city.

- Winters typically aren't cold and snowy. People play golf all year round! The city gets only 8 to 13 inches of precipitation a year—about the same as Los Angeles—and Denver boasts it gets more sunshine than San Diego.

DID YOU KNOW?

Denver gets over 300 days of sunshine a year.

Ready to Cheer?

Coloradans love their sports teams and there's no better place than Denver to join the fun, no matter what the season:

- The Colorado Rockies baseball team plays home games in the heart of downtown Denver in Coors Field from Apr to Sept (2001 Blake St., Denver, CO; 303-292-0200; colorado rockies.com).

- The Denver Broncos football team plays at Sports Authority Field at Mile High (13655 Broncos Parkway, Englewood, CO; 303-649-9000; denverbroncos.com). On game days from Sept to Jan, you'll see everyone wearing team colors orange and blue!

- The NBA's (National Basketball Association) Denver Nuggets play at the Pepsi Center from Oct to Apr (1000 Chopper Circle, Denver, CO; 303-405-1100; nba.com/nuggets).

- The Colorado Avalanche hockey team, the "Avs" to their fans, also play at the Pepsi Center from Oct to Apr (1000 Chopper Circle, Denver, CO; 303-405-6144; coloradoavalanche.com).

DID YOU KNOW?

Denver is home to seven professional sports teams and six new stadiums. Philadelphia is the only other city to root on so many pro teams.

- The Colorado Rapids soccer team calls the high-tech Dick's Sporting Goods Park their home and has players from around the world on their roster (6000 Victory Way, Commerce City, CO; 303-727-3500; coloradorapids.com).

- The Colorado Mammoth is part of the growing National Lacrosse League and play home games in the Pepsi Center. They often attract crowds as big as those who come to see the Nuggets and Avalanche. Their season runs from Dec to Apr (1000 Chopper Circle, Denver, CO; 303-405-1101; coloradomammoth.com).

- The Denver Outlaws play outdoor lacrosse at Sports Authority Field at Mile High from May to Aug (1701 Bryant St., Ste. #700, Denver, CO; 720-258-3623; denveroutlaws .com).

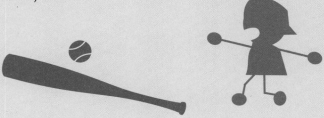

TELL THE ADULTS:

There's a lot to do in and around Denver that's free—or nearly free:

Bring the skateboards to Denver's massive SkatePark (2205 19th St., Denver, CO; denverskate park.com).

Walk the Mile High Trail in City Park. It goes for 3.1 miles! You'll also find baseball, football, and soccer fields; two playgrounds; two lakes; and more (17th Ave. and Colorado Blvd., Denver, CO; denvergov.org/parks).

Explore 850 miles of bike routes and trails (denver .org/things-to-do/sports-recreation/bike-trails).

Float on an inner tube or kayak at Confluence Park (2250 15th St., Denver, CO; 720-913-1311). Rent from Confluence Kayaks, which also rents bikes (2373 15th St., Denver, CO; 877-298-1292).

Visit the US Mint (320 W. Colfax Ave., Denver, CO; 303-405-4761; usmint.gov), where you can learn how money is made!

Hike at the Red Rocks Amphitheatre and Park, famous around the world as a concert venue (8300 W. Alameda Pkwy., Morrison, CO; 720-865-2494; redrocksonline.com).

Take a tour of the Colorado Capitol Building, especially the tour of Mr. Brown's Attic, which includes a children's interactive space (200 E. Colfax Ave., Denver, CO; 303-866-2604; colorado.gov/capitoltour).

Check out the dinosaur foot-prints and dinosaur bones at Dinosaur Ridge, an outdoor museum (16831 W. Alameda Pkwy., Morrison, CO; 303-697-3466; dinoridge.org).

A COLORADO KID SAYS:
"I ride bikes on the bike trails in Denver with my dad whenever it is nice out."
—Emilee, 8, Denver

{ **WHAT'S COOL?** The 32-foot-tall statue of the "Blue Mustang" at the entrance to Denver International Airport, especially at night with its brightly lit red eyes.

GAME ON!

Many sports teams get their names from things relevant to the areas they come from! Use the pictures below to help you name the Colorado sports teams mentioned in this chapter.

2

Sculptures, Paintings & Colorado History

GOT YOUR BACKPACK?

Not your school backpack! These are special backpacks you can borrow at the Denver Art Museum (100 W. 14th Ave. Pkwy., Denver, CO; 720-865-5000; denverartmuseum.org).

With these free backpacks you can build a totem pole, decorate a guitar, or live like a Chinese scholar as you explore the art museum's many exhibits. Become a detective as you look for clues in the furniture gallery or create an American Indian horse mask. This museum is famous for its American Indian collection.

The Denver Art Museum may just be the most kid-friendly art museum in the country. Just looking at the building when you arrive is fun!

A VISITING KID SAYS:
"I really liked the Denver Art Museum because it seemed to be really based around kids."
—Henry, 11, Minneapolis, MN

Besides the backpacks, you can check out art tubes with more activities, stop in the Drawing Studio where you can sketch or paint, or in the Just for Fun Center, play with the giant dollhouse of the museum—complete with what you'd find in the exhibits.

One of the most fun things about this museum is that there are kids' activities everywhere. Look for pictures of the museum's monkey mascot Seymour, who points you to the games on every floor. You can create a creature puppet and tell a story inspired by the artist Hieronymus Bosch, famous for his fantastic images of creatures.

DID YOU KNOW?

The Denver Art Museum is the biggest art museum between Kansas City and the West Coast.

{ **What's Cool?** Checking out a free backpack with art projects at the Denver Art Museum (100 W. 14th Ave. Pkwy., Denver, CO; 720-865-5000; denverartmuseum.org).

Make and mail your own postcard in the western American art gallery or try embroidering or weaving in the European and American Textiles exhibit. Make your own landscape in the Western Art Creation area or decorate a treasure chest with Peruvian animals in the Spanish Colonial exhibit.

This neighborhood is called the Golden Triangle Museum District. That's because besides the art museum, there is:

- The US Mint (320 W. Colfax Ave., Denver, CO; 303-405-4761; usmint.gov), which offers free tours to see how coins are made. Make a reservation in advance!

- The History Colorado Center, where you'll learn the stories of those who came from around the world to build Colorado (1200 Broadway, Denver, CO; 303-447-8679; historycoloradocenter.org).

A COLORADO KID SAYS:
"I like the Material World exhibit at the Denver Art Museum because I love to see what people can do with interesting and different materials."
—Hannah, 11, Denver

- The Kirkland Museum of Fine & Decorative Art, which showcases Colorado artists and thousands of objects from around the world (1311 Pearl St., Denver, CO; 303-832-8576; kirklandmuseum.org).

- The Molly Brown House Museum, where you'll be introduced to this amazing Coloradan and the era in which she lived (1340 Pennsylvania St., Denver, CO; 303-832-4092; mollybrown.org).

DID YOU KNOW?

The famous gold-leaf dome of the Colorado State Capitol (200 E. Colfax Ave., Denver, CO; 303-866-2604; colorado.gov) contains 200 ounces of gold, a reminder of Colorado's gold mining history. Take a tour of the dome!

■ The Clyfford Still Museum, which exhibits Still's work. He was considered one of the most important painters of the 20th century, though most of his abstract works weren't seen for many years (250 Bannock St., Denver, CO; 720-354-4880, clyffordstillmuseum.org).

If you love art, you'll also want to visit the Museum of Contemporary Art, a short distance away (1485 Delgany St., Denver, CO; 303-298-7554; mcadenver.org).

You won't want to leave!

DID YOU KNOW?

The Denver Public Library downtown (10 W. 14th Ave., Denver, CO; 720-865-1111; denverlibrary.org) is one of the biggest libraries in the country. There's a great kids' library here with lots of fun programs!

Art Isn't Just in Museums in Denver!

Did you see the giant *Blue Bear*? He's peering into the Colorado Convention Center downtown (700 14th St., Denver, CO; denverconvention.com). Denver is famous for its public art—like the *Blue Bear*. You'll find murals, sculptures, and all kinds of public art throughout the city in parks, police stations, recreation centers, and more. It's all part of Denver's Public Art Program (artsandvenuesdenver.com/public-art).

What's your favorite?

- *The Metal Flowers* (Chaffee Park, W. 44th St. and Tejon St.)

- *Wynken, Blynken and Nod* (Washington Park at South Downing St. and E. Louisiana)

- *Children's Fountain* (City Park bordered by Colorado Blvd., 17th St., York St., and 23rd Ave.)

- The *Bear* sculpture (at the entrance to the Denver Museum of Nature & Science, 2001 Colorado Blvd., Denver, CO; 303-322-7009; dmns.org)

- *The Laughing Escalator* sound sculpture (Colorado Convention Center)

- *The Bronco Buster* (at Civic Center Park; Bannock St. south of Colfax Ave.)

What Do You See?

When you are at an art museum, you'll have a lot more fun if you do more than simply look at the pictures and sculptures:

- Ask those you're with what's the first thing they've noticed in the painting. Everyone probably has zeroed in on something different!

- Stand in front of the art and pose—like the people, animals, and shapes in the art.

- Make up a story about what you see.

- Imagine what you would hear, or smell, if you were in the art.

The Unsinkable Molly Brown

Do you think you're unsinkable? Molly Brown became known as the Unsinkable Molly Brown because she helped others to survive after the sinking of the *Titanic*. Later, back home in Denver, she became an outspoken advocate for miners' rights and the minimum wage.

She was born poor in Missouri but became rich when her husband, a Colorado mining engineer, discovered gold. They bought a big house in Denver in the Capitol Hill neighborhood. You can visit and learn more about Molly Brown and the times when she lived at the Molly Brown House Museum (1340 Pennsylvania St., Denver, CO; 303-832-4092; mollybrown.org).

A COLORADO KID SAYS:
"My favorite thing to do in Denver is visit the historic Molly Brown House. It allows you to relive one young girl's life story. Denver is full of interesting history and almost anyplace you go there is some significant piece of history linked to it!"
—Delaney, 12, Denver

Ready to Time Travel?

You will at the History Colorado Center, where there's even a time machine that helps you explore what life was like in different parts of Colorado in different eras (200 Broadway, Denver, CO; 303-447-8679; historycolorado.org). All you have to do is push it across the giant Colorado map on the floor. Visit Keota, a 1920s Plains farm town, and see what it was like for kids growing up there. Enroll in the high school, check out the outhouse (no one had bathrooms in those days here!), climb into the hayloft and slide down, and "drive" a Model T to a picnic.

Choose whether to be a military explorer, a mountain man, or a Latina fort employee as you play an interactive computer game exploring what life was like at Bent's Fort on the US/Mexico border and within the homelands of American Indian tribes long before Colorado became a state. At the time, the trading post was the busiest place between Missouri and New Mexico!

DID YOU KNOW?

There were originally three separate towns with three different names on the current site of Denver.

The Ute Indians have lived in Colorado longer than anyone else. They were here before Spanish explorers arrived in 1600. Today, two Ute tribes live in Colorado.

Head "underground" in a mine and see how you would do placing explosives. Walk into the bare quarters at the Amache-Granada Relocation Center, one of the internment camps where Japanese-American families were forced to live during World War II, leaving their homes on the West Coast behind.

Don't miss the *Resilience* exhibit that shows you the challenges the Utes have faced—not the least from white settlers—and how they have survived.

Check out Jumping for Joy. It's hard to believe but the huge Colorado snow sports industry started with small ski-jumping competitions in Steamboat Springs. How good a ski jumper would you be? Thanks to technology, here's your chance to try!

A COLORADO KID SAYS:
"My favorite museum in Denver is the History Colorado Center because they have really interactive exhibits where you can do stuff like collect (wooden) eggs from (not real) chickens."
—Zooey, 11, Denver

TELL THE ADULTS:

Touring cities isn't only about famous sites and museums—especially in Denver. Leave a lot of time to explore the city's neighborhoods and the nearby mountains, to hike or bike, and to cheer on Denver's sports teams. Most important, get the kids involved in the planning:

Let them help plan the itinerary starting at the official Denver tourism website (denver.org) and Colorado website (colorado.com). In winter, check out coloradoski.com, the online guide for Colorado's snow resorts.

Colorado Parent (coloradoparent.com) offers a calendar of kid-friendly activities.

Take a virtual tour of museums and tourist sites before you visit and decide where you want to focus your attention. If you plan to go to many of the city's major museums and attractions, consider getting a MILE HIGH Culture Pass (denver .org/things-to-do/mile-high-culture-pass) that gives you discounted admission to top museums and attractions as well as other discounts.

If the kids are old enough, encourage each to plan a day or half day of your visit. At the very least, make sure each person in the family has a say in the itinerary.

DID YOU KNOW?

Coins last a lot longer than bills—30 years as compared to just 18 months for paper money.

The Denver Mint produces about 7.5 billion coins each year.

Ditch the Car

It's easy to get around downtown Denver without one, especially since the new Union Station Transit Center has opened. You can get most places by walking, or on a bike, light rail, or bus often faster than in a car, and some of the transportation is even free:

- The Free MallRide makes stops at many downtown landmarks along the famous 16th Street Mall and the city Business District including the Colorado State Capitol, Denver Art Museum, the Denver Performing Arts Complex, and the US Mint (rtd-denver.com/unionstation -freemallride.shtml).

- The Free Metroride offers rush-hour service between Union Station and Civic Center Station with stops along 18th and 19th Streets.

- All bus stops have red and white signs that list each bus route that stops there (rtd-denver.com).

- Take the Light Rail to Elitch Gardens Theme and Water Park, the Sports Authority Field at Mile High to see the Broncos or Outlaws, or to the Pepsi Center to see the Nuggets or Avalanche play.

MAKE YOUR OWN MASTERPIECE

You've had the chance to see what other artists have to offer—now it's your turn to get creative! Use the space below to draw your own original work of art!

{ **What's Cool?** Learning the stories of Denver's historic landmarks as you pass by them. Download a free app from iTunes or check out denverstorytrek.org.

3
Dinosaurs, Elephants, Climbing Mountains & Blasting Off to Mars

The "Fourteeners" are the mountains like Mount Evans just west of Denver that are more than 14,000 feet high!

Relax if you don't think you're up to the challenge. We're not really going to climb Mount Evans. Here at Expedition Health at the Denver Museum of Nature & Science (2001 Colorado Blvd., Denver, CO; 303-322-7009; dmns.org), we're going to go along on an interactive expedition—choose your own guide to the top and learn about living in high altitude.

Get a Peak Pass that you plug into the various interactive stations and see how you'd do by taking a muscle challenge. Stop at Biology Base Camp where you can test the sugar content in cereals and see how your face might look when you're 70. Check out how a granola bar looks as it goes through your digestive system. Gross!

DID YOU KNOW?

Locals say the best view in Denver is just outside the Denver Museum of Nature & Science, which also makes it the best place for a family photo or a selfie—with the Denver skyline and the Rocky Mountains as the backdrop.

At another computer station, play a Traumas on the Trail game. Did you know there are 206 bones in your skeleton? You can see your skeleton in front of one screen as you move.

In another museum exhibit, can you carve out shapes in the water that look like photos from Mars? There's a huge Discovery Zone where you can do that, conduct experiments in the Science Kitchen, and more. There's a lot to see at this museum—wildlife exhibit scenes that make you think you're seeing walruses, beavers, and wolves in the wild, and another exhibit that lets you explore how Native American families lived.

A VISITING KID SAYS:
"I like visiting the [botanic] gardens in spring when everything is in bloom."
—Ellie, 12, San Diego, CA

Colorado, of course, was founded on mining, and you can follow a mine shaft into a Colorado mine in the Gems and Minerals area. See the 15-pound gold nugget named "Tom's Baby."

Say hi to the two women who lived in Egypt 3,000 years ago and now make the museum their home. They're mummies, of course, and see what scientists have been able to tell us about them using X-rays and CT scans.

Did you know duckbill dinosaurs were good parents? They laid eggs in the nest, took care of babies, and traveled in groups. Check out the dinosaur eggs in the museum's Prehistoric Journey where you travel through time starting 3.5 billion years ago.

DID YOU KNOW?

The Denver Parks department grows so many flowers for the city's flower-beds that they would stretch for 56 miles if laid out in a straight line. You can see hundreds of plants native to Colorado at the Denver Botanic Gardens (1007 York St., Denver, CO; 720-865-3500; botanicgardens.org).

Touch a fossil, feel a mastodon's tooth, or watch paleontologists and trained volunteers at work behind a big glass wall in their lab.

Now that you've traveled back in time, blast off into the future at Space Odyssey, where you can explore the universe with all kinds of fun interactive activities.

Ready to land on Mars?

DID YOU KNOW?

A 13-year-old girl once found the fossil of a giant Allosaurus dinosaur in Colorado. Dinosaur bones have been found right around Denver! Just 20 minutes outside of Denver, see hundreds of dinosaur footprints and a quarry of bones at Dinosaur Ridge (16831 W. Alameda Pkwy., Morrison, CO; 307-697-3466; dinoridge.org).

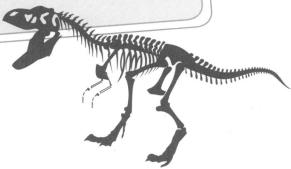

{ **What's Cool?** The big interactive Omni Globe at the Denver Botanic Gardens that shows you the impact of climate change (1007 York St., Denver, CO; 720-865-3500, botanicgardens.org).

Star Lingo

How would you like to visit Mars?

You can at the Denver Museum of Nature & Science's Space Odyssey exhibit and learn more about the cosmos at the Planetarium. But first you've got to learn the lingo:

- Astronomy is the study of space.

- The atom is the simplest building block of the universe.

- A comet is a small icy object from the outer part of the solar system.

- An extraterrestrial is any object, living or not, that originates from some place other than Earth.

- An extremophile is an organism that has adapted to survive in extreme environments.

- A galaxy is a massive collection of stars and celestial objects bound together into a single system by gravity.

- A meteorite is a stony or metallic object from space that survives a fiery entry into the Earth's atmosphere and lands on the surface.

- A solar system is a group of planets, moons, asteroids, comets, and other small objects that orbit one star.

Giant Teddys and Mini Trains

You'll find those along with furnished dollhouses, tiny trains, planes, and cars—even a mini circus and all kinds of dolls at the Denver Museum of Miniatures, Dolls and Toys that's in a historic house at the edge of Denver City Park (1880 Gaylord St., Denver, CO; 303-322-1053; dmmdt.org).

Make a reservation for afternoon tea—with lots of yummy eats—at the museum's Oak and Berries Tea Room. See if there are any kids' workshops when you visit. Ready to make your own miniature castle?

A COLORADO KID SAYS:
"The Denver Museum of Miniatures, Dolls and Toys is my favorite museum in Denver. It's great if you like American Girl dolls like me."
—Dakota, 7, Denver

Flower Power

Yucca plants are not yucky! They're plants that are native to the Southwest, and you'll see a lot of them at the Yuccarama as soon as you enter the Denver Botanic Gardens (1007 York St., Denver, CO; 720-865-3500; botanicgardens.org).

There are 41 individual gardens here: water gardens with indoor waterfalls; the tropical conservatory with its 2-story model of a banyan tree that lets you see what a tropical forest looks like; the Victorian Secret Garden; a meandering waterway with lilies; and the herb garden with more than 150 varieties. Ask the staff here about growing herbs at home!

There's the Mordecai Children's Garden where you can hunt for bugs in the Grasslands or race pinecones down Springmett Stream. Don't miss the Rooftop Alpine Garden! There are also classes and activities for kids and families.

You'll like the birds and bees walk that was designed to attract bees, butterflies, and hummingbirds.

Come in spring to see the wildflowers in the alpine garden and in summer when so much is blooming and you might also catch a concert.

Count how many flowers here you'd never seen!

Snow Mastodon

It was just a normal workday until . . . the bulldozer opera-
tor in Snowmass, Colorado, discovered the bones of a young
Ice Age creature. That was just the beginning, in October
2010. In the months following that first discovery, the Denver
Museum of Nature & Science excavated a treasure of well-
preserved Ice Age fossils—the largest fossil excavation it had
ever undertaken. Museum crews uncovered 5,000 bones of 41
kinds of Ice Age animals—even camels who lived here then.

Some were huge: The Ice Age Columbian mammoths that
lived in Colorado were up to 13 feet tall and weighed 10 tons.
Their relatives, the American mastodons, were just a little
smaller—up to 10 feet tall and weighing up to 8 tons.

This is one of the most important fossil discoveries ever
made in Colorado. Today, there's a Snow Mastodon Discovery
Center in Snowmass Village (snowmastodon.com).

DID YOU KNOW?

The largest known set of dinosaur tracks
found anywhere in North America is in
Picketwire Canyon, in the southeast part of
Colorado (southeastcolorado.com/picketwire).

Talk to the Animals

Can you roar like a lion?

Maybe you'd rather swing like a monkey! At the Denver Zoo, here's your chance to watch the animals—nearly 4,000 of them—giraffes, bears, penguins, elephants, orangutans and monkeys, even vampire bats—and see how they're different and similar to you (2300 Steele St., Denver, CO; 303-376-4800; denverzoo.org). See what special activities are offered when you visit and make sure to catch some of the animal feedings! It's hard to believe this amazing zoo started with just one black bear cub that was given to the mayor of Denver as a gift.

Ready to meet the elephants? Take a stroll through the Toyota Elephant Passage. It's one of the biggest elephant habitats in North America! Besides the elephants, look for greater one-horned rhinos, clouded leopards, and more.

Maybe it's time to go to Africa. At least it will seem like Africa at Predator Ridge where you wander through native brush to meet lions, hyenas, and African wild dogs. Listen to their wailing hoots. That's how they keep the pack together!

Everyone loves the apes and monkeys at the Primate Panorama. Watch the tree-dwelling

monkeys play in their open-air wire-mesh tents 4 stories high. See the gorillas and orangutans roam and climb ropes in their big habitat.

Like snakes? Head to Tropical Discovery where you can greet a python, a Komodo dragon (they're the largest lizards in the world!), and a clownfish, among others.

Denver may be far from the ocean, but you can see a polar bear, seal, and sea lion here at the Northern Shores exhibit. Scientists believe sea lions may be as intelligent as cats and monkeys.

You'll have fun at Bird World with 200 species of birds, including African penguins, flamingos, and bald eagles.

Bear Mountain is based on where bears live in the wild. You'll like this part of the zoo because you'll also find the carousel, Pioneer Train, and Sheep Mountain here.

Of course there are tigers—and leopards. You'll find them at the Felines exhibit.

Maybe you prefer hippos. You can see them and black rhinos at Pachyderms.

Make sure to take a selfie with the bronze mother hippo and calf statue!

TELL THE ADULTS:

City Park is huge—330 acres—the largest park in Denver (17th Ave. and Colorado Blvd., Denver, CO; denvergov.org/parksandrecreation).

Besides the Denver Zoo and the Denver Museum of Nature & Science, there are gardens, two lakes, a boathouse, tennis courts, a golf course, and a huge playground.

Especially on weekends, come early and pack a picnic! And before heading to a place with so much to see and do:

Take a virtual tour of the museum and zoo and decide with the kids what the must-see attractions are.

DID YOU KNOW?

Astronauts have to exercise for 2 hours every day in space to combat the loss of muscle strength because there is so little gravity. They can also move equipment that weighs hundreds of pounds with their fingertips!

Make sure everyone has a say in the itinerary!

Bring snacks and reusable water bottles.

Check to see if there are any special family activities going on. The Denver Museum of Nature & Science, for example, has a large children's Discovery Zone, IMAX movies, planetarium shows, and interactive features throughout its exhibits (dmns.org/exhibition). The Denver Zoo has a special sea lion show, a demonstration at the Elephant Passage, and opportunities to watch different animals being fed (denverzoo.org/plan-your-visit/feedings-showtimes). Most importantly, leave when the kids—and you—have had enough.

A COLORADO KID SAYS:
"I like the space exhibit at the Denver Museum of Nature & Science, especially trying to park the spacecraft in its spot."
—Parker, 10, Denver

Preserve, Guard & Protect

That's what conservation is all about. The Denver Zoo supports more than 600 conservation projects around the world. But there is a lot you can do to protect animals and our planet:

- Turn off lights when you leave a room.

- Turn off the television if no one is watching it.

- Create a recycling center in your home and recycle newspapers, glass, and aluminum cans.

- Turn off the water while brushing your teeth.

- Use both sides of a piece of paper.

- Plant wildflowers in your garden instead of picking them from the wild.

- Reduce the amount of trash you create: Reuse your lunch bag each day.

- Don't buy animals or plants taken illegally from the wild or that are native to your area. Ask where they're from.

- Share what you know with family and friends.

NAME THOSE PLANETS

Can you name all the planets of our solar system?
Unscramble the letters below to uncover all eight!

CMYERUR   _____

NUSEV   _____

TAREH   _____

SRMA   _____

PTIEJRU   _____

SNURTA   _____

NAURSU   _____

PENUNTE   _____

See page 162 for the answers!

A COLORADO KID SAYS:
"The planetarium at the Denver Museum of Nature & Science makes you feel like you're in the stars."
—Riley, 10, Denver

4

Elitch Gardens:

Coasters, Water Rides & More

READY TO SHAKE, RATTLE, AND ROLL?

Board the giant swing at Elitch Gardens Theme and Water Park that turns you upside down as you go round and round (2000 Elitch Circle, Denver, CO; 303-595-4386; elitchgardens.com).

There are 13 thrill rides at Denver's downtown theme park including Boomerang, the steel coaster, Mind Eraser, where your feet are dangling as you go more than 50 miles per hour, and Sling Shot, which launches you in the air.

Of course Elitch Gardens is a lot more than thrill rides. There's a lot of history here. Denver was just 30 years old when Elitch Gardens opened in 1890, and over the years, it was home to Denver's first orchestra, first children's museum, and first movie theater.

DID YOU KNOW?

You can sign up to snorkel with the fish at the Downtown Aquarium in Denver (700 Water St., Denver, CO; 303-561-4450; aquariumrestaurants.com).

Today it's a must-see stop for Denver families and those visiting over the summer and fall when the park stays open on weekends until after Halloween.

There are plenty of family rides including the Big Wheel giant Ferris wheel that's over 100 feet tall, the historic Carousel, the Dragonwing that makes you feel like you are flying, and the Tilt-A-Whirl. Compete with your parents on Ghost Blasters as you make your way through the interactive haunted house. Whoever blasts the most ghosts wins. There are plenty of kids' rides too for the littlest parkgoers (and their older brothers and sisters!), including the Goofy Gazebo with tubes, slides, nets, and ball pits.

A COLORADO KID SAYS:
"I like to ride every roller coaster at Elitch Gardens."
—Alyssa, 14, Denver

What's Cool? The free summer concerts at Elitch Gardens Theme and Water Park (https://elitchgardens.com/concerts).

Elitch Gardens is in a part of Denver called the Central Platte Valley. Besides the theme and water park, there's a huge Greenway ideal for bike rides and picnics, the Downtown Aquarium, the Children's Museum, and nearby, the stadiums where the Denver Broncos, Denver Nuggets, and Colorado Avalanche all play.

At Elitch Gardens, there are also summer concerts and "dive-in movies" at the Water Park. Float in the wave pool while you watch! There are magic shows, dance performances, and even Science Live experiments. Check the schedule when you arrive so you don't miss any of the fun!

Bring a change of clothes! There's the Disaster Canyon raft ride and Shipwreck Falls (ready to plunge over a 50-foot waterfall?) at Elitch Gardens and then all varieties of water slides at the adjacent water park that's included in park admission.

DID YOU KNOW?

The cheeseburger was invented in Denver—when a man named Louis Ballast grilled a slice of cheese on a burger at his Denver drive-in restaurant. Ice cream sodas also were invented in Denver.

Maybe you want to try the Acapulco Cliff Dive—the 65-foot-high speed slide. There's Cannonball Falls, enclosed aqua tubes, and Castaway Creek, where you float down a "river" with geysers and waterfalls. There's a giant wave pool called Commotion Ocean and two more tube slides called Gangplanks.

The only hard part is deciding where to go first!

A COLORADO KID SAYS:
"I like hanging out with my friends at Elitch Gardens. We have a blast!"
—Mac, 11, Denver

Downtown Aquarium

Ready to dissect a squid? You can if you sign up to become a marine biologist for a day at the Downtown Aquarium in Denver (700 Water St., Denver, CO; 303-561-4450; aquariumrestaurants.com).

There's plenty to do here, even if marine biology isn't your thing. There are creatures from North America, the desert, the coral reefs, the rainforest (did you know 7 percent of the world is covered by rainforest?), barrier reefs that run parallel to coastlines, and areas that replicate the edge of the coral reefs, where most shipwrecks occur.

A VISITING KID SAYS:
"My favorite thing we did in Denver was to go to the aquarium and see the really cool octopus."
—Brett, 10, Washington, DC

For the Littlest Museumgoers

The Children's Museum of Denver (2121 Children's Museum Dr., Denver, CO; 303-433-7444; mychildsmuseum.org) is the place where little kids can learn about the plants and animals in their backyards, paint with edible paint, build and launch a rocket, play at the life-sized marble run, design trucks, construct helicopters, and blow giant bubbles. All of these exhibits are geared for kids up to 8, and there's a special area for babies and toddlers. But if you think this all sounds like fun for older kids, you're right! (*Note the museum is undergoing a big expansion that will be completed in the fall of 2015.*)

DID YOU KNOW?

There are mermaids at the Downtown Aquarium in Denver. They're actually young women dressed as mermaids who swim among the sea life while teaching you about the importance of taking care of the environment. Catch their show when you visit.

Scary Rides

Elitch Gardens is famous for its thrill rides. Are you tall enough?

No standing on tiptoes! The height rules are there to keep you safe. Don't make yourself do something you're really scared about. That's no fun!

If you get motion sick, skip rides that have a lot of sharp curves. Take a virtual tour of the park before you go to see what rides you want to go on—and which you would rather skip (elitchgardens.com).

Remember, you don't have to ride any attraction you're not comfortable with! And there's always next time.

DID YOU KNOW?

You can see the Denver Skyline and the Rockies when you ride the Brain Drain thrill ride at Elitch Gardens. It's seven stories high!

Theme Park Smarts

Theme parks are big places. Set up a meeting place just in case some of you get separated. Have your parents write down the name of your hotel, the phone number, and their cell phone numbers in case you get separated (you probably know their cell number—but in case you forget). If you do get separated from your parents, look for someone in a theme park or police uniform. They can help you find your family!

Put your name and contact numbers on your cameras and backpacks. If you misplace them, you're more likely to get them back!

A VISITING KID SAYS:
"Talking to people while waiting on line helps make the time go faster."
—Ginny, 8, Orlando, FL

TELL THE ADULTS:

How about some outdoor fun?

Denver's Central Platte Valley is less than a mile west of downtown and right where you find attractions including the Children's Museum of Denver, Downtown Aquarium, Elitch Gardens, and the stadiums where the Broncos, Avalanche, and Nuggets play.

You can:

Learn a little history along the Greenway Trail, a paved bike trail that follows the South Platte River for almost 30 miles. The Colorado Historical Society has erected more than 20 large historic signs that tell the story of the area, from where dinosaurs roamed to where Native Americans lived to the wildlife and birds.

DID YOU KNOW?

With less water vapor in the air at this high altitude, the sky really is bluer in Denver.

Colfax Avenue in Denver is the longest continuous street in the USA—26 miles.

Gear up for outdoor adventures at the REI flagship store here in a restored 1901 building with its indoor climbing wall. You can rent camping gear here or sign up for a class (1416 Platte St., Denver, CO; 303-756-3100; rei.com/stores/denver.html).

Hop on the Platte Valley Trolley on weekends from May to Oct at the Children's Museum or the Downtown Aquarium for a tour, with stops at the major attractions along the way (303-458-6255; denvertrolley.org).

Kayak, bike, or have a picnic. Rent from Confluence Kayaks (2373 15th St., Denver, CO; 303-433-3676; confluencekayaks.com).

A VISITING KID SAYS:
"I always have snacks in my backpack at a theme park."
—Amber, 11, Los Angeles, CA

Bug Hunt

Bugs or butterflies?

You'll see plenty of both at the Butterfly Pavilion and Insect Center just 15 minutes from Denver in Westminster (6252 W. 104th Ave., Westminster, CO; 303-469-5441; www .butterflies.org).

All of the creatures here are invertebrates, animals without backbones.

There are more than 1,600 butterflies in the Wings Over the Tropics conservatory. Watch them emerge from their chrysalides.

You aren't anywhere near a tide pool in Colorado, but you can touch live sea stars, horseshoe crabs, and other aquatic invertebrates from the Atlantic and Pacific Oceans at the touch tank.

Ready to go eye-to-eye with a tarantula or a scorpion? Maybe you'd rather take a hike on the Nature Trail and check out the native habitats. This is a great place for a bug hunt!

DID YOU KNOW?

The vast majority of animals are invertebrates—like butterflies. That means they have no backbone.

FILL IN THE MISSING LETTERS

Fill in the missing letters in the names of the fun rides, games, and attractions you can find at Elitch Gardens.

1) M _____ nd Er _____ ser

2) G _____ ofy Ga _____ ebo

3) Shi _____ wreck F _____ lls

4) B _____ g Whe _____ l

5) D _____ agon _____ ing

6) Sli _____ g S _____ ot

7) B _____ ome _____ ang

8) Gh _____ st B _____ asters

See page 162 for the answers!

{ **What's Cool?** Holding Rosie, a Chilean Rose Hair tarantula, in your hand at the Butterfly Pavilion and Insect Center (6252 W. 104th Ave., Westminster, CO; 303-469-5441; www.butterflies.org).

5

Souvenirs, Burritos, Farmers' Markets & Corn Mazes

BRONCOS OR ROCKIES T-SHIRT?

Maybe you'd rather get a sweatshirt that says "Colorado," a bracelet that was made here, or a dream catcher to hang in your room (they're a Native American tradition that's supposed to protect you from bad dreams).

Got your souvenir money? You've got lots of choices.

Stroll down the famous 16th Street Mall (1001 16th Street Mall, Denver, CO; 303-534-6161; 16thstreetmall denver.com). It was designed by I. M. Pei, the world-famous architect who also designed the Louvre Pyramid in Paris and a lot of other famous buildings.

You won't dodge cars here—it's only for pedestrians. There are lots of restaurants and shops. You'll find stores selling everything from western souvenirs (like dream catchers!) to clothes, shoes, and more.

Check out Larimer Square nearby (1430 Larimer St. #200, Denver, CO; 303-534-2367; larimersquare.com). Maybe you're in the market for real cowboy boots? It's fun to just people-watch here too!

DID YOU KNOW?

Coloradans like to put green chile sauce on burritos, tamales, enchiladas, and other food. It's made from green and red chiles, spices, and often, chunks of pork. Sometimes it is really spicy!

Up in Boulder, it's fun to people-watch along the 4-block-long Pearl Street Mall that's also just for pedestrians (1942 Broadway St. #301, Boulder, CO; 303-449-3774; boulderdowntown

.com). Grab an ice cream or frozen yogurt and browse along with the students who attend the University of Colorado here. You'll find local stores as well as brands you know. Can you find something you can't get at home?

A lot of families head to the Cherry Creek neighborhood to Denver's big Cherry Creek Shopping Center (3000 E. 1st Ave., Denver, CO; 303-388-3900; shopcherry creek.com) and lots of other shops nearby.

Remember farmers' markets aren't just for food. You'll find lots of crafts at the farmers' markets in Denver, Boulder, and in historic mountain towns like Breckenridge, only about an hour and a half from Denver (gobreck.com).

All that shopping probably made you hungry, and you've got plenty of choices—farmers' markets where locals whip up specialties and places for burgers, pizza, and sushi. But just like you don't want to bring home a souvenir that you could get anywhere, try some new food in Colorado—maybe something that comes from a local farm or ranch or from Colorado's Native American and Hispanic traditions.

Ever had a tamale?

{ **WHAT'S COOL?** Picking out the fixings for a picnic—at a local farmers' market. Visit coloradofarmers.org.

And for Dessert!

- Liks Ice Cream (2039 E. 13th Ave., Denver, CO; 303-321-2370; liksicecream.com) is famous for its homemade ice cream in umpteen flavors.

- Boulder Baked (1911 Broadway St., Boulder, CO; 303-444-4999; boulderbaked.com) has great cupcakes and cookies.

- Santa Fe Cookie Co. (303 16th St. #12A, Denver, CO; 303-623-0919) is in the heart of downtown. Just put a dollar in the jar and grab your cookie!

- Little Man Ice Cream (2620 16th St., Denver, CO; 303-455-3811; littlemanicecream.com) is housed in a 28-foot-tall cream can, and you can get ice cream served in a homemade waffle cone.

- Rocky Mountain Chocolate Factory (500 16th Street Mall and locations through-out Denver Metro, Denver, CO; 303-629-5500; rmcf.com) is famous for their huge caramel apples as well as chocolates.

Song and Dance

The Denver Center for the Performing Arts is the country's second biggest with 10 theaters. It's home to the Colorado Symphony Orchestra, Opera Colorado, the Colorado Ballet, and it is also where big Broadway hits are performed. There are a lot of programs for families—including more than 20 productions aimed at kids, Colorado Symphony, Family Concerts, ballet performances of *The Nutcracker* at the holidays, and classes for kids during school breaks (1101 13th St., Denver, CO; 303-893-4100; denvercenter.org).

DID YOU KNOW?

The 16th Street Mall is pedestrian only—for all 17 blocks! There are free shuttle buses along the way.

Colorado is known as the Centennial State because it became a state in 1876—28 days after the country's 100th birthday.

Souvenir Smarts

- Look for something that you can buy only in Colorado—something with the state flag or a mountain peak, for example.

- Consider if you want one big souvenir or several smaller things to add to a collection like pins, patches for your backpack, or stickers that you could put on your water bottle.

- Resist impulse buys.

A VISITING KID SAYS:
"My recommendation for a souvenir is something you can use every day that will remind you of the trip, like a keychain."
—Alexia, 8, San Diego, CA

Shop 'Til You Drop

- I Heart Denver (Level 2 of Denver Pavilions, 500 16th Street #264, Denver, CO; 720-317-2328; iheartdenver.info), right on Denver's 16th Street Mall, is the place to get a souvenir that was made in Colorado by local crafters and artisans. Pick up a deck of cards with all of Colorado's highest mountains or handcrafted wooden toys and support the local economy.

A COLORADO KID SAYS:
"I like to go shopping at the Cherry Creek Mall."
—Maddie, 10, Denver

- Talulah Jones (1122 E. 17th Ave., Denver, CO; 303-832-1230; talulahonline.com) sells toys and games that are eco-friendly.

- Tattered Cover Book Store (1628 16th Street Mall, Denver, CO, and various other locations around Denver; 303-436-1070; tatteredcover.com) has an expansive children's section with books arranged in a way that makes browsing enjoyable.

- The Wizard's Chest (230 Fillmore St., Denver, CO; 303-321-4304; wizardschest.com) is housed in a castle and inspired by J. R. R. Tolkien's *Lord of the Rings* trilogy and brings fantasy to life. Stop by to play a board game!

- Into the Wind (1408 Pearl St., Boulder, CO; 800-541-0314; intothewind.com) has every color and shape of kite you can imagine, as well as other great toys to take to the park or on a camping trip, like boomerangs, Frisbees, and yo-yos.

- Where the Buffalo Roam (1320 Pearl St. Front, Boulder, CO; 303-938-1424; focuscorporation.com/wherethebuffaloroam .html) is a great one-stop souvenir shop for picking up a CU Boulder T-shirt, a Buffs stuffed animal, or a Colorado mug, especially if you have some University of Colorado Buffs fans in the family.

DID YOU KNOW?

The Tattered Cover Book Store downtown is one of the country's premier bookstores (1628 16th Street Mall, Denver, CO; 303-436-1070; tatteredcover .com). (Look for the satellite stores at the Denver International Airport.)

Festivals Are Made for Kids

Whenever you visit, check to see if there is a special festival or fair. They've always got lots of fun things for kids—and parents—to do:

- JANUARY—The National Western Stock Show, including one of the nation's largest rodeos (nationalwestern.com)

- MARCH—St. Patrick's Day Parade, the city's largest annual parade (denverstpatricksdayparade.org), and Denver March Powwow featuring more than 1,500 dancers from close to 100 tribes (denvermarchpowwow.org)

- MAY: Cinco de Mayo Festival, one of the largest in the country with arts and crafts, mariachi bands, and more (cincodemayodenver.com), and the Downtown Denver Festival of the Arts (denverartsfestival.com)

- JUNE—Denver Chalk Festival when hundreds of artists transform Larimer Square with works made out of pastel chalk (larimerarts.org), and the Juneteenth Music Festival that celebrates African-American culture (juneteenthmusicfestival.com)

DID YOU KNOW?

Olde Town Arvada, part of the Denver metro area, has a Festival of Scarecrows every October, with dozens displayed all around town (historicarvada.org).

- JULY 4—Fireworks throughout the city (visitdenver.com), and Buffalo Bill Days, which celebrate the great western performer with a Wild West Show, parade, and more in Golden, Colorado (buffalobilldays.com)

- AUGUST—The Denver County Fair, complete with skateboard rodeo and carnival (denvercountyfair.org)

- SEPTEMBER—A Taste of Colorado with food from dozens of Colorado restaurants, carnival rides, and music over Labor Day weekend (atasteofcolorado.com)

- OCTOBER—Boo at the Zoo with special Halloween festivities at the Denver Zoo (denverzoo.org)

- NOVEMBER—Denver Arts Week, which celebrates all the arts including a special free Night at the Museums (denver artsweek.org)

- DECEMBER—The Blossoms of Light at the Denver Botanic Gardens, complete with carolers (botanicgardens.org), and Zoo Lights holiday festivities at the Denver Zoo (denver zoo.org)

TELL THE ADULTS:

Denver is a great place to encourage kids to try new foods, whether with a picnic of goodies bought at a local farmers' market or at an ethnic restaurant or upscale eatery that welcomes junior foodies. Don't be shy about asking if you can order a half or appetizer portion. Here are some places popular with kids and adults alike:

Casa Bonita (6715 W. Colfax Ave., Lakewood, CO; 303-232-5115; casabonitadenver.com) is a Denver landmark and much more than just a Mexican restaurant. There's a 30-foot indoor waterfall and pool where a team of cliff divers entertain, puppet shows, and a big gift store.

The Fort (19192 CO 8, Morrison, CO; 303-697-4771; thefort.com) is next to the red rocks in a traditional adobe fort. The food is based on what pioneers ate on the historic Santa Fe Trail and is the place to try buffalo, elk, duck, quail, and pheasant, but picky eaters and vegetarians can easily find other options.

What's Cool? Trying a new dish on vacation—and loving it!

Steuben's (523 E. 17th Ave., Denver, CO; 303-830-1001; steubens.com) is in a sleek converted garage in the Uptown neighborhood. It's known for comfort food, wholesome kids' meals, and plenty of options for those with food allergies.

Steve's Snappin' Dogs (3525 E. Colfax Ave., Denver, CO; 303-333-7627; stevessnappindogs.com) is home of the Denver Dog, wrapped in a tortilla and filled with chili and other fixings, and the Mex-Si Dog, which starts with a hot dog that is wrapped in bacon and then fried. There are kids' meals and plenty of vegetarian options.

The Snooze, an A.M. Eatery (2262 Larimer St., Denver, CO, and locations throughout Denver Metro; 303-297-0700; snoozeeatery.com) is an excellent choice for breakfast. Try the Molten Chocolate Lava Pancakes and the Breakfast Pot Pie.

Cherry Cricket (2641 E. 2nd Ave., Denver, CO; 303-322-7666; cherrycricket.com) is one of the best places in town for burgers. Build your own with the list of more than 30 toppings!

Eating Smart on Vacation

Vacations are a good time to try different foods other than just what is on a kids' menu. That's especially true in Denver where you'll find every variety of food and plenty that is grown locally. Here's how you can eat healthier and try new foods:

- Split a portion of something else with your brother or sister, or your mom or dad.

- If there is something you like on the grown-up menu, ask if you can get a half portion or order an appetizer size.

- Opt for fruit as a snack instead of chips or candy.

- Visit and talk to the farmers at the farmers' markets.

- Drink water rather than a soda. Your reusable bottle becomes a souvenir when you put stickers on it from all the places in Denver you've been!

DID YOU KNOW?

The Denver Omelet really was invented in Denver with green peppers, onions, and ham. Many people believe it began as a western sandwich with the same ingredients prepared by Chinese cooks while working on the railroads.

SECRET WORD DECODER

Using the key, write the letters under the symbols to figure out the secret phrase. Clue: Art doesn't always have to be hung in a museum. Visit here and you might find it right beneath your feet!

For example:  = b i r d

_ _ _ _ _ _   _ _ _ _ _

_ _ _ _ _ _ _ _

a= ✔   b= 🚲   c= 🏙   d= ✈   e= 🎁

f= 🏭   g= 🏛   h= 🏠   i= 🛣   j= 🏠

k= 🌿   l= ?   m= ❗   n= 👁   o= 🚤

p= 🌲   q= 🏔   r= 🚇   s= ✦   t= 🏟

u= 📢   v= 📦   w= 🚩   x= 🔈   y= ❤

z= 💐   .= ◼   != 🚌   ,= 🛶

See page 162 for the answers!

6

Boulder:
Flatirons, Tubing,
Bike Rides & Farmers' Markets

TIME TO JOIN THE CROWD

Strap on your helmet and hop on a bike in Boulder! You've got your pick of 300 miles of bike and hiking trails, many that you can reach from most streets downtown, including the Boulder Creek Path that winds through town for more than 5 miles. Plenty of places have kids' bikes and helmets for rent too.

Maybe you'd rather hike in Eldorado Canyon State Park (9 Kneale Rd., Eldorado Springs, CO; 303-494-3943; parks.state.co.us) where you might see a golden eagle or a red-tailed hawk. Rock climbers come here to scale the high granite walls.

Go to Chautauqua Park (9th St. and Baseline Rd., Boulder, CO; 303-413-7200; https://bouldercolorado.gov/parks-rec/chautauqua-park) above Boulder to climb the city's famous Flatirons. The views are worth it!

DID YOU KNOW?

Thirty thousand students attend the University of Colorado in Boulder, which is also home to Naropa University, the country's only Buddhist university.

{ **What's Cool?** Boulder's free Apocalypse Skate Park (7483 Arapahoe Rd., Boulder, CO; sk8parklist.com/co_apoc.html). Don't forget your helmet!

In summer you can tube or kayak in and around Boulder; in winter, you can snowshoe, cross-country ski, down-hill ski, or snowboard nearby at Eldora Mountain Resort (861 Eldora Ski Rd. #140, Eldora Mountain Resort, Nederland, CO; 303-440-8700; eldora.com).

Try fly fishing in Boulder Creek or convince your parents to start the day with a hot air balloon ride. Boulder has always been forward thinking and geared to the outdoors.

You can stand-up paddleboard or canoe in the Boulder Reservoir (5565 N. 51st St., Boulder, CO; 303-441-3461; https://bouldercolorado.gov/parks-rec/boulder-reservoir), where there's also plenty of hiking and biking trails.

Boulder began as a mining town. Railroads began to connect Boulder to other major areas, and in the 1870s, the population tripled. Nearly from the beginning, the community preserved land for public use. That's why there are so many places to play outside.

But there's more than outdoor fun here—just ask a student who goes to the University of Colorado. The campus is beautiful! And even though this is a small city, there are several museums that welcome kids with plenty of hands-on activities and special camps.

DID YOU KNOW?

The Boulder Creek Path goes right through historic downtown and follows along Boulder Creek. Bicycling is so highly regarded in Boulder—most people own bikes here—that sometimes the city plows the Boulder Creek bike path before they plow the streets.

Of course you've got to leave time for shopping! The Pearl Street Mall (942 Broadway St. #301, Boulder, CO; 303-449-3774; boulderdowntown.com)—no cars allowed!—is a good place to souvenir shop and people-watch too. Unlike a lot of other places, most of the shops here are locally owned.

Buy a kite, a new pair of hiking shoes, or a toy to bring home for your dog. Check out the street performers!

A COLORADO KID SAYS:
"It's really fun to go biking along the bike trails in the mountains. I really love when you get to bike next to a river!"
—Olivia, 11, Denver

Downtown is also the place to catch an outdoor concert, chat up the farmers at the big farmers' market, or get something good to eat. Ever had a buffalo burger?

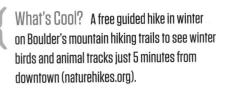

What's Cool? A free guided hike in winter on Boulder's mountain hiking trails to see winter birds and animal tracks just 5 minutes from downtown (naturehikes.org).

It Pays to Be Green

Got a reusable water bottle?

It will become a souvenir when you slap stickers on it from all the places you've visited in Colorado. And you'll be helping the planet.

You'll be helping too when you take public transportation, walk, or ride a bike rather than drive from place to place.

Here are some other simple things you can do to help the environment:

- Turn off the lights and air conditioner when you leave where you are staying

- Recycle

- Reuse towels

- Take shorter showers

DID YOU KNOW?

People in Boulder take being green seriously. Their taxes support open space. You'll see cars that are fueled with bio-diesel and shops along the Pearl Street Mall are wind powered. The Wi-Fi is solar powered!

Tea Time

The young entrepreneurs started by harvesting fresh herbs from the Rocky Mountains, drying and blending them, and sewing them into muslin bags. They thought herb tea could help people be healthier.

Today, Celestial Seasonings is one of the biggest specialty tea manufacturers in North America, traveling around the world to find the best natural ingredients for their teas. They serve more than 1.6 billion cups of tea every year. You can stop and take a free tour in Boulder at Celestial Seasonings Tea Company (4600 Sleepytime Dr., Boulder, CO; 303-581-1202; celestialseasonings.com). Take a sniff in the Mint Room and check out the teapot collection in the Art Gallery. Ready to sample the newest flavor?

A COLORADO KID SAYS:
"Make sure to go on the Celestial Seasonings Tea Tour in Boulder. There is a dress made completely out of tea and the peppermint room smells delicious!"
—Jamie, 10, Denver

A Little Culture, A Lot of Fun

Boulder's festivals are as much fun for kids as for grownups and a chance to learn something new:

- Colorado Shakespeare Festival (277 UCB, Boulder, CO; 303-492-8008; coloradoshakes.org), where many performances are under the stars at the University of Colorado's Mary Rippon Theater (Jun–Aug).

- Colorado Music Festival (900 Baseline Rd., Boulder, CO; 303-449-1397; comusic.org)—a 7-week celebration showcasing Beethoven, Mozart, Strauss, and more each summer (June–Aug). Check out the new Music Discovery Garden!

- Boulder Creek Festival with live entertainment, art exhibits, handcrafted items, street performers, and more. Held in the Boulder Creek/downtown area, Memorial Day weekend (bouldercreekfestival.com).

- Chautauqua Park Historic District hosts the Silent Film Series, the Colorado Music Festival, local art exhibits, guided nature hikes, concert performances, and more just for families (900 Baseline Rd., Boulder, CO; 303-442-3282; chautauqua.com).

Local Boulder museums are great for kids:

- The amazing western art at the Leanin' Tree Museum of Western Art. Admission is free (6055 Longbow Dr., Boulder, CO; 303-530-1442; leanintreemuseum.com).

- Learn about global warming at the National Center for Atmospheric Research in Boulder, where you can also see how lightning is created (1850 Table Mesa Dr., Boulder, CO; 303-497-1000).

- Summer weeklong workshops for kids at the Boulder Museum of Contemporary Art (1750 13th St., Boulder, CO; 303-443-2122; bmoca.org).

- Family programs and summer kids' workshop at the University of Colorado Museum of Natural History (16th and Broadway, Boulder, CO; 303-492-6892; http://cumuseum .colorado.edu).

- Hands-on activities at the Boulder History Museum (1206 Euclid Ave., Boulder, CO; 303-449-3464; boulderhistory.org).

TELL THE ADULTS:

Boulder is considered one of the country's "foodiest" towns with nearly 500 restaurants for its 100,000 people, many show-casing menus that use local and seasonal ingredients. It's a great place to let kids experiment with food and for the grownups to try a local brew or wine (bouldercoloradousa.com/things-to-do/brewery-winery-distillery-tours)—there are nine breweries, five wineries, and two distilleries in town!

A COLORADO KID SAYS:
"Colorado is an amazing place to be outdoors. You won't get bored!"
—Leslie, 11, Aspen

Boulder Sliced and Diced: A Chef's Guide for Visitors—offers itineraries from local chefs for enjoying Boulder and the good eats here (boulder slicedanddiced.com).

Boulder Farmers' Market—The Boulder Farmers' Market is the place to eat local, talk to local chefs and farmers, and pick up picnic fixings. The market is open Sat May 4 to Oct 4 (8 a.m.–2 p.m.) and on Wed afternoons (4–8 p.m.). There is live music and beer and wine (downtown on 13th Street between Canyon and Arapahoe; boulderfarmers.org).

Foolish Craig's for breakfast (1611 Pearl St., Boulder, CO; 303-247-9383; foolishcraigs.com).

Tea or dinner at Boulder Dushanabe Teahouse along the Boulder Creek in a unique building (1770 13th St., Boulder, CO; 303-442-4993; boulderteahouse.com).

Abo's for pizza (1124 13th St., Boulder, CO; 303-443-3199; abos pizza.com).

Juanita's for Mexican (1043 Pearl St., Boulder, CO; 303-449-5273; juanitas-boulder.com).

Boulder Café to try a buffalo burger, fondue pasta, or more while the kids watch the street performers on the Pearl Street Mall. There's also a kids' menu (1247 Pearl St., Boulder, CO; 303-444-4884; bouldercafeonpearl.com).

WORD SEARCH: TALK LIKE A SKATER

At first, they called it "sidewalk surfing"—putting skate wheels on the bottom of wooden boards—and it started in Southern California among surfers. Today there are more than 150 skate parks in Colorado—from Aspen to Boulder to Denver to Steamboat Springs—and skate shops around the state too. (Visit coloradoskateboardguide.com.) You don't want to be a *poser*—someone who looks like a skater but doesn't really know anything. Here are some things to remember if you want to sound like you know what you are talking about at the skate park:

You are a *skater*, not a skateboarder.

Deck isn't what's in the backyard; it's the wooden part of your skateboard.

Sick means something is really cool. So does *gnar* (short for gnarly).

Sketchy is something that isn't well done, like a sketchy trick.

Bailing is when you either fall or jump off your board before falling.

Getting air is when you get all four wheels of your skateboard off the ground and into the air.

Pop has nothing to do with soda; it's a skating maneuver that involves tapping the tail (or the back) end of the board to the ground so that the board *pops* upward.

Ollie is achieved by "popping" the tail on the ground and using the front foot to even out your body and get "air."

CIRCLE THE SKATER TERMS!

Skater
Sick
Sketchy
Air
Ollie

Deck
Gnarly
Bail
Pop
Poser

```
A  L  A  B  D  T  G  M  G  S  I  C  K
S  K  A  T  E  R  N  U  V  S  E  T  O
B  O  S  M  C  E  O  E  U  E  G  R  A
E  T  R  O  K  L  P  R  P  O  P  U  P
R  M  E  C  T  M  O  B  N  L  H  I  R
U  I  A  N  L  I  S  R  R  L  T  E  F
B  E  G  N  A  L  E  U  I  I  K  O  D
A  B  R  Z  B  O  R  H  M  E  S  S  N
I  R  O  Y  O  C  C  O  L  A  E  K  S
L  N  M  O  R  A  H  U  M  L  T  E  B
J  U  D  M  G  N  A  R  L  Y  N  T  C
Y  F  D  N  C  W  I  T  Q  L  E  C  S
E  C  V  Y  T  N  R  E  E  W  R  H  B
G  A  I  R  M  E  U  S  O  N  I  Y  A
```

See page 163 for the answers!

7

Gold Panning, Mountain Hikes & Garden of the Gods

NATURAL WONDER OR MAN-MADE?

In Colorado Springs, the state's second biggest city, you can take your pick—from natural wonders like Garden of the Gods with its giant sandstone cliffs, to the historic Pikes Peak Cog Railway you can ride to the top of the mountain (take the Santa Train at the holidays!), to the spectacular modern Cadet Chapel at the US Air Force Academy.

This area has been home to Native Americans, gold miners,

A COLORADO KID SAYS:
"Go visit Garden of the Gods in Colorado Springs because the big rocks are red and orange."
—Leah, 10, Colorado Springs

mountain climbers, and those coming to the dry, mild climate to improve their health. These days, people still come to enjoy the outdoors but also to go to college, serve in the military, and even train for the Olympics (visitcos.com).

Thank Spencer Penrose for the adventures you can have at the Cheyenne Mountain Zoo. He made his fortune at the nearby gold mine and started the zoo with his collection of animals that originally were kept at the huge Broadmoor Hotel, which he also built. The Broadmoor is famous for its holiday light displays and family activities (1 Lake Ave., Colorado Springs, CO; 719-623-5112; broadmoor.com).

Come to Wild Nights at the zoo (4250 Cheyenne Mountain Zoo Rd., Colorado Springs, CO; 719-633-9925; cmzoo.org/exploreLearn/groupPrograms/animal Encounters.asp) to see what the animals do at night or sign up for a special animal encounter to get to know your favorite animal—elephants, giraffes, lions?

DID YOU KNOW?

Colorado is famous for historic railroads including the most famous, the Pikes Peak Cog Railway, outside Colorado Springs in Manitou Springs—the highest cog in the world, carrying passengers to the famous summit of Pikes Peak at 14,115 feet. You can also hike, bike, or drive to the top.

Zebulon Montgomery Pike was just a young Army lieutenant when he first saw what later would be named after him. He called it Grand Peak and, a few years later, he tried to climb to the top. Even though he didn't make it, his account of that 1810 expedition literally put the Colorado mountain on the map, and it's been called Pikes Peak ever since.

One of the largest gold strikes in history—more than half a billion dollars worth of gold—was dug from Cripple Creek near the base of Pikes Peak. But "The Springs," as locals call Colorado Springs, was never a

DID YOU KNOW?

The highest zoo in the country is in Colorado Springs—the Cheyenne Mountain Zoo (4250 Cheyenne Mountain Zoo Rd., Colorado Springs, CO; 719-633-9925; cmzoo.org).

typical boomtown. It always attracted those coming for their health, writers, inventors, entrepreneurs, and artists. Colorado College, a private liberal arts school, was founded here in 1874. Learn more about the pioneers who settled this area at the free Colorado Springs Pioneers Museum (215 S. Tejon St., Colorado Springs, CO; 719-385-5990; cspm.org).

The US Air Force Academy was built here in the 1950s, and today there are five big military installations here where thousands of people work.

A COLORADO KID SAYS:
"It's fun to go hiking in the summer because it's fun to see all the different flowers."
—Lauren, 10, Denver

{ **What's Cool?** The wildflowers you'll see on the M. Walter Pesman Trail outside of Denver. Take a summer hike with a guide from the Denver Botanic Gardens (720-865-3533; botanicgardens.org).

You may bump into an Olympian while you're here. Hundreds come to train because the US Olympic Committee is headquartered here along with its flagship training center for athletes in sports including basketball, volleyball, fencing, and gymnastics (750 E. Boulder St., Colorado Springs, CO; 719-866-4618; teamusa.org).

The one place you won't want to miss is Garden of the Gods. People come from all over the world to hike and rock climb amid the 300-foot-high red sandstone rock formations (805 N. 30th St., Colorado Springs, CO; 719-634-6666; gardenofgods.com). Make sure you've got your camera!

A COLORADO KID SAYS:
"Definitely go to the Olympic Training Center in Colorado Springs."
—Valeria, 11, Colorado Springs

What's in Your Backpack?

When you're going hiking, Colorado kids say you need:

- A reusable water bottle filled with water—two if you are going on a long hike! Put stickers on it and it becomes a souvenir.

- A rain jacket and an extra layer of clothes.

- Lunch and snacks. Make your own trail mix to bring!

- A phone to take pictures and keep in touch in case you get separated from your parents.

- Band-Aids.

- Magnifying glass.

- Sunscreen (you need it even if it's cloudy!).

- Bandana.

A COLORADO KID SAYS:
"If you're visiting Denver, you should visit the Rocky Mountains. I always have warm clothing and water in my backpack when I'm hiking."
—Evan, 10, Denver

US Air Force Academy

The Air Force Academy in Colorado Springs is both a military organization and a university. Much of the academy is set up like most other Air Force bases, particularly the 10th Air Base Wing with more than 3,000 military and civilian people. But the academy is also a university where 4,400 students study. To attend, you must be nominated by your congressman or senator. Once accepted, students become members of the US Air Force and will serve on active duty after they graduate. Most of their professors are Air Force officers. Though the academy was founded in 1954, women weren't accepted until more than 20 years later. You can visit the academy (2346 Academy Dr., Air Force Academy, CO; 719-333-2025; usafa .edu). Make sure to see the Cadet Chapel, famous for its 17 spires that are more than 150 feet high! You can also see it from I-25.

DID YOU KNOW?

The US Air Force Academy Drum and Bugle Corps performs around the world, including at Presidential Inaugural parades, the Macy's Thanksgiving Day parades, and the Tournament of Roses parades.

Bison, Moose & Hawk!

Colorado is home to seven National Wildlife Refuges. Different from national parks and always free, National Wildlife Refuges were created to conserve America's wildlife across the country and in Colorado are a good place to spot wildlife—everything from bison to moose to bald eagles and hawks (fws.gov/refuges). Check out the Let's Go Outside! website for kids (fws.gov/letsgooutside/kids.html) where you can play online games, learn how to help fish and wildlife, and find out how to have the most fun outdoors at a Wildlife Refuge:

- See what lives under a dead tree.

- Try to match animal tracks.

- Have a scavenger hunt with your family.

- Close your eyes and listen—to nature!

- Start a nature journal, writing down or taking pictures of the wildlife you see.

TELL THE ADULTS:

The outskirts of Denver are wonderful to explore. Here are some favorite day trips.

Mount Evans and Echo Lake: You can drive on the highest paved auto road in the country from Memorial Day through the beginning of Oct (west on I-70 to Idaho Springs and take the Mount Evans exit [#240], mountevans.com).

Central City and neighboring Blackhawk once was called the "Richest Square Mile on Earth." Now the mining towns from the 1870s are a good bet for mine tours and the chance to try gold panning in streams where a half billion dollars was found (visitor center at 103 Eureka St., Central City, CO; 303-582-3345; blackhawkcolorado.com and central citycolorado.us).

The Lariat Loop is a 40-mile National Scenic Byway drive less than 30 miles from Denver that connects Golden, Morrison, Lookout Mountain, and Evergreen and includes attractions like the Colorado Railroad Museum, Red Rocks Amphitheatre, Historic Golden, and Dinosaur Lookout (lariatloop.org).

South Park/Fairplay is known for some of the best fishing in Colorado; the chance to see antelope, mule deer, and elk; and ghost towns (southparkcity.org). Don't miss the homemade tamales at Dorothy's (123 Frontage Rd., Fairplay, CO; 719-836-9120), where you can bowl while you're eating!

Royal Gorge and Canon City Royal Gorge Bridge & Park feature the world's largest suspension bridge, spanning the Arkansas River. Admission includes a real tram trip, and there's also the chance for a ride on the world's steepest incline railway to the bottom of the gorge (4218 County Rd. 3a, Canon City, CO; 888-333-5597; royalgorgebridge.com).

DID YOU KNOW?

The highest paved road in America is the road to Mount Evans (off of I-70 from Idaho Springs). It climbs up to 14,258 feet. No wonder there's often snow on the road in summer.

Gold!

Maybe you'll get lucky. Gold is still being found in Colorado. Here's where you can do some of your own gold panning:

- Mollie Kathleen Gold Mine (9388 Hwy 67, Cripple Creek, CO; 719-689-2466; goldminetours.com) is named after the first woman to strike gold in Colorado. You descend 100 stories underground! You're guaranteed a gold nugget at the end of the tour.

- Hidee Gold Mine Tour, where you can chip away at a gold vein and keep what you find and pan for gold (720 Hidee Mine Rd., Central City, CO; 720-548-0343; hideegoldmine .com).

- Country Boy Mine Tour, where you slide down a 55-foot-long chute and pan for gold (542 French Gulch Rd., Breckenridge, CO; 970-453-4405; countryboymine.com).

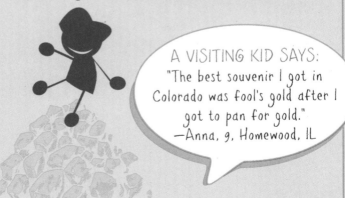

A VISITING KID SAYS:
"The best souvenir I got in Colorado was fool's gold after I got to pan for gold."
—Anna, 9, Homewood, IL

CONNECT THE DOTS!

Many people were drawn to the West by the possibility of finding gold and making a fortune. Connect the dots to draw a gold miner!

8

Rocky Mountain National Park:

Moose, Elk, Starry Nights & Wildflowers

WANT TO FEEL LIKE YOU'RE ON TOP OF THE WORLD?

You can if you drive "the highway to the sky" in Rocky Mountain National Park. That's what people call Trail Ridge Road because it is so high—over 12,000 feet at its highest point.

You may start in a forest of aspen trees, but in a just few minutes, you're above the treeline in conditions you'd find in the Arctic. Bring a jacket. It will be 30 degrees colder up here and too cold for trees to grow. But look closely and you'll see all kinds of tiny plants. Watch for hawks and eagles flying by.

A COLORADO KID SAYS:
"There is lots of great wildlife at Rocky Mountain National Park. Last time we were there we saw a moose!"
—Abel, 12, Denver

Many hiking trails branch off from Trail Ridge Road. Just be careful to stay on the trails as you hike! The tundra is very fragile. It could take the plants hundreds of years to recover from being trampled.

Rocky Mountain National Park is one giant outdoor playground! There are more than 350 miles of hiking trails. Let's not forget 114 mountain peaks and 147 lakes all within the park!

If you visit in spring, don't miss the big waterfalls. It's the snowmelt that swells the rivers and makes waterfalls roar in the spring. This preserves a huge watershed that not only nourishes life here but provides water for people living downstream.

DID YOU KNOW?

There's a Native American legend explaining why leaves change color in fall: Great Bear smelled a hunter's fire. The bear and the hunter fought, spattering yellow cooking grease and red blood on the leaves of the aspen trees.

You'll pass through the town of Estes Park if you enter the park from the east, Grand Lake if you come in from the west.

You can buy all kinds of souvenirs—from Christmas tree ornaments to summer T-shirts to stuffed animals—as well as anything you've forgotten to bring from home. Check out the big old Stanley Hotel up on a hill in Estes Park (333 Wonderview Ave., Estes Park, CO; 970-557-4000; stanleyhotel.com). At one time, it was the fanciest resort in the Rockies and was the inspiration for Stephen King's horror novel *The Shining*.

Many families gather for big reunions in Estes Park at the YMCA of the Rockies (2515 Tunnel Rd., Estes Park, CO; 888-613-9622; ymcarockies.org).

Archaeologists think that ancient Native American families came here for some summer fun more than 10,000 years ago. Later the Ute and the Arapahoe tribes came here to hunt. Today families come to camp

and hike in summer, cross-country ski and sled in winter, fish for trout, and, of course, see the elk, moose, bighorn sheep, and some 280 bird species that make this one of the best wildlife-watching destinations in the whole country.

Glacier Gorge Junction is one of the most popular areas for a walk in the wilderness. Hike 2.5 miles from the trailhead there to Mills Lake or take a hard 5.3-mile hike to Andrews Glacier.

DID YOU KNOW?

In May, golden eagle chicks hatch in nests all over Rocky Mountain National Park, which is home to 10 pairs of golden eagles. There is also a pair of bald eagles that nests just outside the park.

If your family is in really good shape and you are feeling good in high altitude, you might be able to climb Flattop Mountain at 12,324 feet, which has beautiful views along the way. Rocky Mountain National Park is home to one of Colorado's famous "Fourteeners," Long's Peak, which is the tallest mountain in northern Colorado at 14,259 feet. That is a very difficult 12-hour hike that might better wait until you are older. For information about Long's Peak, check out nps.gov/romo/planyourvisit/longs peak.htm.

Keep your water bottle filled!

A COLORADO KID SAYS:
"We go to Rocky Mountain National Park in the fall to see the elk."
—Archer, 12, Denver

Elk

The Shawnee name for elk is Wapiti. It means "white rump."

Colorado has North America's largest elk herd—260,000. Thousands of elk spend their summers on the lower edge of the tundra in Rocky Mountain National Park, but then, when it gets cold, move to lower elevations like Horseshoe Park, Moraine Park, Kawuneeche Valley, and Beaver Meadows. At dusk, you might see them grazing in the meadows. Check out those antlers! The antlers on a bull elk can weigh 25 pounds and span 5 feet. The elk grows a new set of antlers every year. If you visit in fall, listen for the elk. Their eerie, loud calls are known as bugles and mean it's time for the mating season.

Come in October for Estes Park's annual Elk Fest (visit estespark.com/events-calendar/special-events/elk-fest). There's even a contest to see who sounds most like an elk!

DID YOU KNOW?

Deer and elk are herbivores (plant eaters). Mountain lions are carnivores (meat eaters). Black bears eat both meat and plants. They're called omnivores. Which are you?

Bear Smarts

Bears may look big and clumsy, but they can run 35 miles per hour—fast enough to catch a horse. They can be very dangerous. Bears usually avoid people but might get angry if you get too close. Black bears live in Rocky Mountain National Park. Here are some tips from the bear experts at Rocky Mountain National Park to keep you safe in bear country:

- In campgrounds and picnic areas, if there is a food storage locker provided, use it.

- Avoid storing food and coolers in your vehicle. If you must, store food in airtight containers in the trunk or out of sight. Close vehicle windows completely.

- Do not store food in tents or pop-up campers in campgrounds or in vehicles at trailheads.

- Food, coolers, and dirty cookware left unattended, even for a short time, are subject to confiscation by park rangers; citations may be issued.

- Dispose of garbage in bear-resistant Dumpsters and trashcans.

- Human-fed bears usually end up as chronic problems and need to be removed. A fed bear is a dead bear.

- In the backcountry, store food, scented items, and garbage in commercially available bear-resistant portable canisters.

- Pack out all garbage.

- Never try to retrieve anything from a bear.

- Report all bear incidents to a park ranger.

- Do not leave pets or pet food outside and unattended, especially at dawn and dusk. Pets can attract animals into developed areas.

- Avoid walking alone.

- Don't run ahead or lag behind on the trail. Talk about what to do if you see a bear. Stay calm! Back away slowly and avoid eye contact. Don't run or make any sudden movements.

A Giant Dividing Line

The Continental Divide Trail runs all the way from Mexico to Canada—3,100 miles! All rivers on the east side of the Divide flow toward the Atlantic Ocean, while those on the west flow toward the Pacific Ocean. In 1803 President Thomas Jefferson bought the Continental Divide, sight unseen, as part of the huge Louisiana Purchase. He immediately sent Captain Meriwether Lewis and his friend William Clark to investigate. Their famous Lewis and Clark Expedition charted the territory clear to the Pacific Ocean, encouraging countless pioneers and settlers to follow.

In Rocky Mountain National Park, you'll cross the Continental Divide at Milner Pass on the winding Trail Ridge Road that's only open weather permitting from late May through mid October. Stop for a picnic or a walk along the way.

You can also stop for a photo op at the Continental Divide Landmark in Colorado in Loveland on US 6 (cdtrail.org). If you're feeling short of breath, it's because you're almost 12,000 feet above sea level.

{ **What's Cool?** The WebRangers site for kids from the National Park Service that lets you build your own ranger station, share pictures, and more (nps.gov/webrangers).

Hiking Smarts

Remember, it's about the journey, not how far you get on a hike. Here are some basic ranger rules to keep safe on the trail:

- Wear sturdy, comfortable shoes with moisture-wicking socks.

- Don't wander off the trail.

- Never hike alone. Keep track of everyone in your group.

- Carry a whistle to blow in case you get separated.

- Don't drink the water in rivers or streams unless you have a certified water purification kit.

- If lightning threatens, stay in a low, crouched position with only your feet touching the ground. Stay away from tall trees.

- Don't jump from rock to rock near the edges of streams.

- Make sure the adults have a first-aid kit.

DID YOU KNOW?

If wild animals get used to human food given to them by summer visitors, they may starve in winter. That's why you should never feed them.

TELL THE ADULTS:

Rangers frequently talk about the animals at evening campfires in different national park campgrounds. They also lead wildlife-watching walks and special family activities. Stop at the parks' visitor centers and ask the rangers about these special programs and pick up a Junior Ranger packet for the kids to complete; maybe they can steer you to some likely spots to find the animals you most want to see. Visit the park's website with the kids in advance and talk about what you want to do while you're there: nps.gov (some national parks have areas on their websites just for kids!). Whichever parks you visit, you're guaranteed a memorable family adventure:

Rocky Mountain National Park (1000 Hwy. 36, Estes Park, CO; 970-586-1206; nps.gov/romo) between Estes Park and Grand Lake is huge—415 square miles! You'll want to spend some time in Estes Park (visitestespark.com), which is considered the gateway to Rocky Mountain National Park. Many families hold reunions at the YMCA of the Rockies.

Mesa Verde National Park is located in southwest Colorado and offers a spectacular look into the lives of the Ancestral Pueblo people who made it their home for over 700 years, from AD 600 to 1300.

Today the park protects nearly 5,000 known archaeological sites, including 600 cliff dwellings. These sites are some of the most notable and best preserved in the US. Mesa Verde is located approximately 35 miles west of Durango and 9 miles east of Cortez off Hwy. 160. For further information, call 970-592-4465 or visit nps .gov/meve.

Great Sand Dunes National Park (visitor center 1999 CO 150, Mosca, CO; 719-378-6395; nps.gov/ grsa) where the tallest sand dunes are 750 feet high—at an elevation of 8,700 feet! You can carve your way down the dunes on sleds—or just point your sled down.

The Black Canyon of the Gunnison (Rim Drive Rd., Montrose, CO; 970-249-1914; nps.gov/blca) in southwest Colorado boasts sheer black walls up to 2,700 feet. People come here to see the wildlife, camp, fish, and in winter, snowshoe and ski. It's a great place for stargazing!

Animal Etiquette

You can't just barge right into an animal's home. You wouldn't do that to your neighbor. You'll have the best luck seeing animals early in the morning or late in the afternoon when they are most active:

- Watch for dens, trails, or holes marked by pine nuts or acorns.

- If you see an animal, move slowly so you don't scare it.

- Always watch from a distance; never approach the animals.

- Never feed the animals.

DID YOU KNOW?

Colorado is a great place to see wildlife! There are four national parks, 300 state wildlife areas, and 960 wildlife species here.

CAN YOU FIND YOUR WAY THROUGH THE
NATIONAL PARK?

9
Summer in Ski Country:
Mountain Bike, Raft, Zipline & Horseback Ride

NOW'S YOUR CHANCE!

You can try something you've never done in Colorado ski towns in the summer—mountain bike down a mountain, zipline high above the trees, whitewater raft, or gallop on a horse.

A lot of people who live in Colorado mountain towns say they came for the snow sports but stayed because summer is so much fun. Their kids think so too!

Of course there's plenty to do if you're not an adrenaline junkie—souvenir shop in the mountain towns, buy the fixings for a picnic at a farmers' market to take to an outdoor concert, hike amid fields of wildflowers, boat on

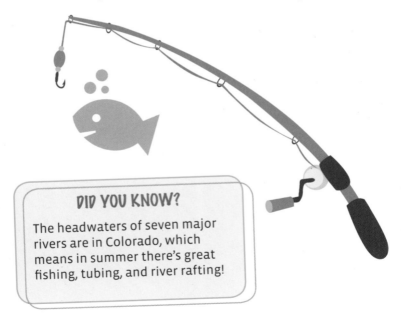

DID YOU KNOW?

The headwaters of seven major rivers are in Colorado, which means in summer there's great fishing, tubing, and river rafting!

a mountain lake, or learn to fly fish. There are plenty of options and many don't cost anything. Go camping!

There are lots of summer camp programs for kids too. You're guaranteed to have fun whether you stay a few days, a week, or all summer as some families do. Here are some ski towns that really roll out the red carpet for kids—and their families:

Vail Resort has Adventure Ridge with a 1,200-foot zipline and adventure ropes courses (600 W. Lionshead Circle, Vail, CO; 970-476-9090; vail.com).

Keystone Resort is one of the closest ski resorts to Denver with a Kidtopia Play Park; the chance to paddle boat, kayak, and canoe on Keystone Village Lake; and Kid's Discovery Days every Tues with special free activities—circus acts, magic shows and more (100 Dercum Sq., Keystone, CO; 970-496-4000; keystoneresort.com).

A COLORADO KID SAYS:
"I like to go camping because you can sleep in a tent."
—Lauren, 10, Denver

Winter Park is just an hour from Denver and is the place to go mountain biking with the Trestle Bike Park, the largest mountain bike park in the US with plenty of kid-friendly trails. You can get up close and personal with sled dogs on a Sled Dog Kennel Tour and Cart Ride or join local kids fishing on the Fraser River Valley Lions Club Ponds (near the Safeway store off of Hwy 40 in Fraser). Winter Park Resort has a climbing wall along with trampoline bungee jumping. Bring your parents to the Tues night free concerts (85 Parsenn Rd., Winter Park, CO; 303-316-1564; playwinterpark.com).

Breckenridge not only has a big Fun Park at its ski resort with a zipline, alpine coaster, and mini golf, but a big public skateboard park, interactive art and music workshops, a mountain bike free ride park, and paddle boating on Maggie Pond (111 Ski Hill Rd., Breckenridge, CO; 970-453-2913; gobreck.com).

Snowmass is one of Aspen's four mountains and is family central; you can sign up for a day or a week at Camp Aspen/Snowmass and go mountain biking, play paintball, and more. Come to the top of the mountain kids' playground at the weekly Valhalla Nights and the Ice Age Discovery Center in the village (Snowmass Tourism, PO Box 5566, Snowmass Village, CO 81654; 970-922-2233; aspensnowmass.com).

Steamboat Springs has a side-by-side alpine slide and three Colorado state parks where you can camp, fish, hike, and water-ski. The Kid's Adventure Zone has the only bumper cars on ice in Colorado (2305 Mt. Werner Circle, Steamboat Springs, CO; 970-879-6111; steamboat.com).

The only hard part is deciding what to do first!

DID YOU KNOW?

You can ride bikes for more than 40 miles on the Rio Grande Trail from Glenwood Springs to Aspen along the Roaring Fork River. It's built on a former rail corridor.

Big Dude

Dude ranches have been around for more than a century. They started as places where adventurous Easterners could get a taste of life on a western cattle ranch.

That's why families still visit, but these days, besides horseback riding, parents and kids fish, raft, hike, and swim in dude ranches across Colorado and the West. Some even have tennis courts and pools. There are plenty of kids' activities, cookouts, cowboy music, and the chance to gallop into the backcountry and sleep under the stars (coloradoranch.com; duderanch.org).

A COLORADO KID SAYS:
"I like to go to Steamboat Springs because it has so many fun things to do during the summer as well as the winter."
—Jessica, 9, Denver

What's Cool? Joining the calf scramble for kids at the weekly rodeo in Steamboat Springs where you try to grab a ribbon off a calf's tail (970-879-1818; steamboatrodeo.com).

Horse Smarts

Colorado is a great place to go horseback riding, whether you're staying on a ranch or just going for an afternoon ride in the mountains. Just remember:

- Horses are big, powerful animals. Be kind to them and respect their strength.

- Know your horse's name and make friends with him.

- Wear boots or shoes with good heels. They should come above your ankle.

- Wear long pants to protect you from getting saddle sores and a hat to keep you from getting sunburned. Don't forget sunscreen.

- Listen to the wranglers. They know their horses and can explain how the horse will respond to you.

- Always approach a horse from the front while talking in a reassuring tone. Don't yell.

- Watch for low-hanging branches, fallen logs, and streams. It's easy to fall off a horse.

Water Smarts

Colorado may be high in the mountains, but there are plenty of places to have fun in the water: lakes; swimming pools; hot springs; and rivers and creeks ideal for tubing, rafting, and kayaking. If you're heading to Colorado in summer:

- Be cautious around lakes and rivers even if you're not swimming. Cold temperatures, currents, and underwater hazards can make a fall dangerous.

- Always swim with a buddy.

- Stay away from pool and hot tub drains where you can get sucked under water.

- Don't dive unless you know the depth of the water and that there are no rocks underneath.

- When boating, even if you're a great swimmer, wear Coast Guard–approved life jackets.

DID YOU KNOW?

You can tube down a hill on the snow in the summer at Keystone Resort's Adventure Point (keystoneresort.com)— in shorts and T-shirt!

Soar Above the Trees

There are nearly two dozen ziplines across Colorado, the *Denver Post* says, many in or near ski country towns. After a safety talk, you're strapped into a climbing harness, clipped onto a pulley, and then . . . you fly high above the trees and the mountains. Kids as young as 5 can go in many places:

- Crested Butte Mountain Resort Zipline Tour (12 Snow-mass Rd., Crested Butte, CO; 970-349-2211; skicb.com).

- Durango Mountain Resort Purgatory Plunge Zipline (1 Skier Place, Durango, CO; 970-247-9000; durango mountainresort.com).

- Tenmile Flyer Zipline at Breckenridge (1599 Ski Hill Rd., Breckenridge, CO; 970-453-5000; breckenridge.com).

- Zip Adventures of Vail (4098 Hwy 131, Wolcott, CO; zipadventures.com).

- Top of the Rockies Zipline (6492 Hwy 91, Leadville, CO; 800-247-7238; topoftherockieszipline.com).

- Royal Gorge Zipline Tours (45045 W. US 50, Cañon City, CO; 719-275-7238; royalgorgeziplinetours.com).

Summer Festival Fun in Ski Country and Beyond

You'll find summer festivals that welcome kids as well as adults all over Colorado ski country (colorado.com):

- The Aspen Eco Fest (aspenchamber.com) in June has more than 100 street vendors and demonstrations, all free to the public from 10 a.m. to 5 p.m. Shop and enjoy everything handmade, remade, natural, organic, up-cycled, or energy efficient!

- Breckenridge (gobreck.com) kicks off summer in June with Kingdom Days, a town-wide heritage celebration that honors the town's mining roots with free activities including outhouse races, gold panning, and live music, and then later in the summer, Breck Bike Week (breckbikeweek.com) has a week of summer fun including guided group bike rides, bike-in movies, and kids' races.

- Crested Butte Wildflower Festival is in July. As the official Wildflower Capital of Colorado, Crested Butte is the obvious place to host this event, packed with guided wildflower hikes, 4x4 tours, photography classes, gardening instruction, and much more (crestedbuttewildflowerfestival.com).

- Greeley Stampede is one of Colorado's largest summer festivals and rodeos, going strong for more than a century over July 4th weekend with kids' rodeo, carnival, parade, and music (greeleystampede.com).

- Colorado Balloon Classic (balloonclassic.com) in Colorado Springs is Colorado's largest hot air balloon festival with massive colorful balloons ascending each morning and torches lighting up the balloons flying in the night sky.

133

TELL THE ADULTS:

Adults and kids with special challenges can have life-changing adventures in the mountains. There are special programs at ski country resorts designed to get them—and their families—outdoors in summer and winter doing everything from canoeing and kayaking to horseback riding, mountain biking, rock climbing, and in winter, skiing and snowboarding. Many volunteers help make these programs happen, and there are sliding scale costs:

The National Sports Center for the Disabled in Winter Park is one of the largest outdoor therapeutic recreation agencies in the world with activities and camps for all ages (Winter Park Resort, 33 Parsenn Rd., Winter Park, CO; 970-726-1518; nscd.org).

The Breckenridge Outdoor Education Center's mission is to expand the potential of people of all abilities through outdoor experiences, including wilderness programs for kids with developmental disabilities and those on the autism spectrum (524 Wellington Rd., Breckenridge, CO; 970-453-6422; boec.org).

Crested Butte Adaptive Sports Center programs can include family and friends with over a dozen outdoor adventure–based activities in and around Crested Butte for people with disabilities. All activities are highly adaptable and can be structured for any skill level or goal (10 Crested Butte Way, Crested Butte, CO; 970-349-5075; adaptivesports.org).

Challenge Aspen in Snowmass, CO, has been an innovator in adaptive recreation with programs that include art and drama as well as outdoor adventure camps (Snowmass Village Mall #309, Snowmass Village, CO; 970-923-0578; challenge aspen.org).

Steamboat Adaptive Recreation Sports (STARS) offers programs and camps during sum-mer for biking, kayaking, fishing, and waterskiing and in winter as well (2200 Village Inn Ct., Steamboat Springs, CO; 970-870-1950; steamboatstars.com).

DID YOU KNOW?

Mountain biking got its start in Crested Butte, CO (visitcrestedbutte.com). Today ski resorts across Colorado open their lifts to those who want to bike down the trails they skied down in winter! Just an hour from Denver, Winter Park has more than 600 trails and calls itself the Mountain Bike Capital of the USA (winterparkresort.com).

A COLORADO KID SAYS:
"I love biking, especially around Aspen and Glenwood Springs."
—Ansley, 8, Aspen

HOW DO YOU MOUNT A HORSE?

Put these steps in order from 1 to 8.

_____	Swing your leg over
_____	Grab the front of the saddle
_____	Hold the reins
_____	Adjust your seat
_____	Pull yourself up
_____	Stand at your horse's side
_____	Slowly sink into the saddle
_____	Put your foot in the stirrup

See page 163 for the answers!

{ **What's Cool?** River rafting in Colorado. It's better than any roller coaster. You fly over crashing rapids, bouncing up and down, holding on to the side of the boat. Just when you think you can't take any more, the river slows and you float lazily along, taking pictures and watching for animals. Ask where you're staying for local outfitters.

10

Fun in the Snow:
Ski, Snowboard, Skate & Tube

THERE'S NO FEELING LIKE IT!

You're flying down a snow-covered mountain on skis or a snowboard, zooming past trees and grownups—and maybe your mom and dad!

That's after you've had a few lessons, of course! Some kids start skiing before they've even gone to kindergarten. They make it seem really easy. But skiing and riding are a lot harder than they look. That's why you shouldn't try to head off on some expert slope before you've learned the correct technique.

Ski schools shouldn't really be called schools because they're so much fun, and they give you the chance to meet kids from all over the world. Together, you'll learn the skills to conquer snow-covered peaks safely.

DID YOU KNOW?

Breckenridge may be a big ski town, but it's the largest historic district in the state of Colorado with 350 historic structures dating back to when it was a mining town.

These days, snow resorts have special just-for-kids areas on the mountains, mascots, as well as activities when the lifts have closed—tubing, ice skating, broomball games, bonfires, snowcat tours, ziplines, big hot tubs, and festivals all winter. You can try something you've never done—take a snowshoe walk on top of Aspen Mountain or soak in the hot mineral springs in Steamboat Springs.

There are plenty of places to have fun in the snow not too far from Denver:

Winter Park (85 Parsenn Rd., Winter Park, CO; 303-316-1564; winterparkresort.com) is where many Denver kids learn to ski and ride.

A COLORADO KID SAYS:
"When I go skiing, I always have a package of hand warmers in my pockets."
—Blake, 9, Denver

Copper Mountain is home to the Woodward Camps, where there are programs winter and summer to help you hone your tricks (209 10 Mile Circle, Frisco, CO; 970-968-2318; woodwardcopper.com, coppercolorado.com).

Aspen/Snowmass boasts four separate mountains—Aspen Mountain (also known as AJAX), Buttermilk, Aspen Highlands, and Snowmass. Families ski on all of them, but kids especially like Snowmass not only because it is the biggest, but also because it is home to the coolest kids' center in Ski Country—The Tree House with its own climbing wall (800-525-6200; aspensnowmass.com).

A COLORADO KID SAYS:
"I like Beaver Creek because there's ice skating, skiing, and good jumps!"
—Mark, 11, Denver

{ **What's Cool?** The special just-for-kids areas through the trees at many Colorado ski resorts. Look for them on trail maps.

Steamboat (2305 Mt. Werner Circle, Steamboat Springs, CO; 970-879-6111; steamboat.com) wants to give you a taste of being in the West in the town and on the slopes. Come for the annual February Winter Carnival!

Vail Resorts operates four separate resorts in Summit County and each has something unique for families:

- Vail, of course, is the largest snow resort in the country with its famous back bowls (800-805-2457; vail.com).

- Breckenridge has plenty of terrain no matter what your level and a historic town that's fun to visit with lots of shops, restaurants, and even a Children's Museum (1599 Ski Hill Rd., Breckenridge, CO; 970-453-5000; breckenridge.com).

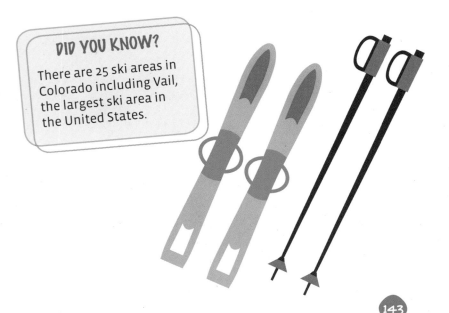

DID YOU KNOW?
There are 25 ski areas in Colorado including Vail, the largest ski area in the United States.

- Beaver Creek Resort has special SpringFest family activities in March and April (40 Village Rd., Avon, CO; 970-754-4636; beavercreek.com).

- Keystone is kid-central not only because kids ski free all season, but because of the daily Kidtopia activities (100 Dercum Sq., Keystone, CO; 970-496-4000; keystoneresort.com).

There are many more ski areas and resorts, small and large, farther from Denver. Check Colorado Ski Country's website for more information (coloradoski.com).

Ready to race?

A COLORADO KID SAYS:
"I like Keystone because there are so many different trails. My favorite is Elk Run."
—Madison, 11, Denver

DID YOU KNOW?

Steamboat Springs has produced a record 79 winter Olympians, more than anywhere else in North America. They call Steamboat "Ski Town USA" (steamboat-chamber.com).

Ski Country Museums

When the weather is too nasty to snow or ride or you just need a break, stop in at a ski country museum:

- Mountain Top Children's Museum in Breckenridge, where you might learn about the animals who live nearby, create art and your own colors, or come at night for a special kids-only program (605 South Park Ave., Breckenridge, CO; 970-453-7878; mtntopmuseum.org).

- The Durango & Silverton Narrow Gauge Railroad and Museum tells you the story of the famous trains that wind through canyons and remote wilderness. You can also take a ride on the railroad (479 Main Ave., Durango, CO; 970-247-2733, durangotrain.com).

- Tread of Pioneers Museum is the place to learn all about Steamboat Springs and its unique snow sports history by going on a scavenger hunt through the museum (800 Oak St., Steamboat Springs, CO; 970-879-2214; treadofpioneers.org).

- The Colorado Ski & Snowboard Museum in Vail will tell you everything you want to know about the history of riding and skiing in Colorado (231 S. Frontage Rd. E., Vail, CO; 970-476-1876; skimuseum.net/visit.php).

Snow Carving 101

Got a big plastic garbage can? A big cardboard box will do.

Fill it with snow and stomp it down really hard. Turn the can upside down and you've got a block of snow. (If you have a box, you can just cut the cardboard away.) Let it freeze overnight and you're ready to become a snow carver.

Get out cheese graters, putty knives, spoons, and paint scrapers—whatever you have will work. Pick an animal shape, a flower, or something else you'd like to build. Use a small toy or a picture to guide you.

See how the pros do it in Breckenridge every January. That's when the International Snow Sculpture Championships are held with teams coming from around the world to compete, creating amazing huge sculptures of giant flowers, butterflies, dinosaurs, and even kids tubing (gobreck.com/events/international-snow-sculpture-championships).

What's your masterpiece going to look like?

DID YOU KNOW?

In southwest Colorado, there is a park exclusively for ice climbers in Ouray. They have a big Ice Festival every January (ourayicepark.com).

Lids on Kids

Got your helmet? A lot of snow resorts insist you wear one when you take lessons to learn to ski or ride because you are safer. You'll stay warmer and drier too with a helmet on your head, and once you slap stickers on it, people will know all the mountains you've seen. Wear your helmet whenever you head out on the slopes. Your parents should wear one too. Check out Lids on Kids for fun games (lidsonkids.org).

Know the Code

Always ski and ride in control.

- The people ahead of you have the right of way. Whenever starting downhill or merging, look uphill and yield.

- Stop in a safe place for you and others, not in the middle of a slope.

- Observe signs and warnings and keep off closed trails.

- Look for the colors on the trail signs: Green trails are easiest; blues are harder, and blacks are for experts. Ski on the trails where you feel the most comfortable. It's more fun.

- Stop when you're tired or cold. That's when people tend to get hurt.

Gear Up

The wrong clothes can ruin a fun day on the slopes. You need:

- Clothing layers, starting with a base layer that will wick moisture away.

- Socks that are made for ski or snowboard boots. Don't wear cotton athletic socks or socks that are too thick.

- Waterproof pants, jacket, and mittens.

- A helmet for skiing or snowboarding—not a bicycle helmet.

- Goggles or good sunglasses. (You'll want goggles if it's snowing!)

- Sunscreen: In the mountains, you're closer to the sun, which is especially strong when it reflects off the snow.

- A healthy snack in your pocket.

DID YOU KNOW?

One of the world's first snow-boards was made in a seventh grade woodshop class. Tom Sims called his 1963 invention a "Skiboard."

Ski Patrol

You can pick ski patrollers out on the mountain by the white cross on their parkas and the first-aid belts around their waists. You'll see them helping skiers who have been hurt or have gotten lost. The National Ski Patrol (nsp.org) makes skiing safer. If you get lost, look for a member of the ski patrol or an instructor with a class. They'll help you.

A COLORADO KID SAYS:
"I like going to Winter Park Resort because it is a great skiing mountain."
—Asher, 10, Denver

Ski patrollers range in age from teenagers to grandparents. Many are volunteers. The National Ski Patrol was founded in the 1930s by New York business-man Charles Minot Dole after he broke his ankle skiing—and had to get down the mountain by himself. The National Ski Patrol has become the largest winter rescue organization in the world, saving many lives. Say thanks next time you see a ski patrol member.

TELL THE ADULTS:

Snow sports are expensive. But lessons are one thing to spend money on. Let the pros teach the kids! They've had special training and know the most fun spots on the mountain. Here are some ways to keep costs down:

Early season and late season often offer the best lodging deals with discounted lift tickets.

Kids 6 and under ski free at resorts including Aspen (aspensnowmass.com) and Crested Butte (skicb .com); kids 5 and under ski free at Steamboat (steamboat.com), Copper Mountain (coppercolorado .com), Winter Park (winterparkresort.com), and some others.

Kids who are in fifth grade are eligible for the Colorado Ski Country USA Ski Passport whether they live in Colorado or not. Kids will get three free lift tickets at most Colorado resorts. Sixth graders get 4 days of skiing for $99. But you must apply in advance (coloradoski.com/passport).

There are many opportunities for discounted and free lessons and lifts in January during Learn a Snow Sport Month (skiandsnowboardmonth.org).

You can save money if you book flights, lodging, and lifts together from companies like ski.com.

SKIER'S LOG

Some ski slopes have the wackiest names! Keep track of the ones you've been down by writing them in the space below!

A VISITING KID SAYS:
"I love snowboarding at terrain parks where you get to go off jumps and on rails."
—Skyler, 12, Washington, DC

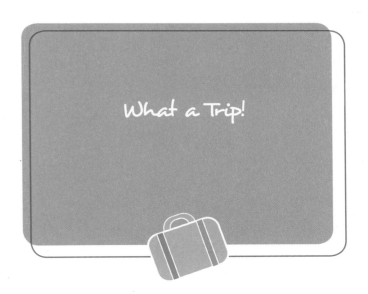

What a Trip!

I came to Colorado with:

_____

_____

_____

The weather was:

_____

_____

_____

We went to:

_____

_____

_____

We ate:

_____

_____

_____

We bought:

_____

_____

_____

I saw these famous Colorado sites:

_____

_____

_____

My favorite thing about Colorado was:

_____

_____

_____

My best memory of Colorado was:

_____

_____

_____

My favorite souvenir is:

_____

_____

_____

_____

_____

_____

_____

WHAT DID YOU SEE?

You had such a great time in Colorado! Draw some pictures or paste in some photos of your trip!

Index

Answer Keys

Astronomy Word Scramble (p. 47)

MERCURY

VENUS

EARTH

MARS

JUPITER

SATURN

URANUS

NEPTUNE

Fill in the missing letters (p. 61)

1) Mind Eraser

2) Goofy Gazebo

3) Shipwreck Falls

4) Big Wheel

5) Dragonwing

6) Sling Shot

7) Boomerang

8) Ghost Blasters

Secret Word Decoder (p. 77)

Denver Chalk Festival

Word Search: Talk Like a Skater (p. 91)

```
A  L  A  B  D  T  G  M  G  S  I  C  K
S  K  A  T  E  R  N  U  V  S  E  T  O
B  O  S  M  C  E  O  E  U  E  G  R  A
E  T  R  O  K  L  P  R  P  O  P  U  P
R  M  E  C  T  M  O  B  N  L  H  I  R
U  I  A  N  L  I  S  R  R  L  T  E  F
B  E  G  N  A  L  E  U  T  I  K  O  D
A  B  R  Z  B  O  R  H  M  E  S  S  N
I  R  O  Y  O  C  C  O  L  A  E  K  S
L  N  M  O  R  A  H  U  M  L  T  E  B
J  U  D  M  G  N  A  R  L  Y  N  T  C
Y  F  D  N  C  W  I  T  Q  L  E  C  S
E  C  V  Y  T  N  R  E  E  W  R  H  B
G  A  I  R  M  E  U  S  O  N  I  Y  A
```

How do you mount a horse? (p. 137)

6 Swing your leg over

4 Grab the front of the saddle

2 Hold the reins

8 Adjust your seat

5 Pull yourself up

1 Stand at your horse's side

7 Slowly sink into the saddle

3 Put your foot in the stirrup

About the Author

Award-winning author Eileen Ogintz is a leading national family travel expert whose syndicated Taking the Kids is the most widely distributed column in the country on family travel. She has also created TakingtheKids.com, which helps families make the most of their vacations together. Ogintz is the author of seven family travel books and is often quoted in major publications such as *USA Today*, the *Wall Street Journal*, and the *New York Times*, as well as parenting and women's magazines on family travel. She has appeared on such television programs as *The Today Show*, *Good Morning America*, and *The Oprah Winfrey Show*, as well as dozens of local radio and television news programs. She has traveled around the world with her three children and others in the family, talking to traveling families wherever she goes. She is also the author of *The Kid's Guide to New York City*, *The Kid's Guide to Orlando*, *The Kid's Guide to Washington, DC*, *The Kid's Guide to Chicago*, *The Kid's Guide to Los Angeles*, *The Kid's Guide to Boston*, *The Kid's Guide to San Diego*, and *The Kid's Guide to San Francisco* (Globe Pequot).